Palgrave Studies in Affect Theory and Literary Criticism

Series Editors
Adam Frank
University of British Columbia
Vancouver, BC, Canada

Joel Faflak
Western University
London, ON, Canada

The recent surge of interest in affect and emotion has productively crossed disciplinary boundaries within and between the humanities, social sciences, and sciences, but has not often addressed questions of literature and literary criticism as such. The first of its kind, Palgrave Studies in Affect Theory and Literary Criticism seeks theoretically informed scholarship that examines the foundations and practice of literary criticism in relation to affect theory. This series aims to stage contemporary debates in the field, addressing topics such as: the role of affective experience in literary composition and reception, particularly in non-Western literatures; examinations of historical and conceptual relations between major and minor philosophies of emotion and literary experience; and studies of race, class, gender, sexuality, age, and disability that use affect theory as a primary critical tool.

More information about this series at
http://www.palgrave.com/gp/series/14653

Erica L. Johnson

Cultural Memory, Memorials, and Reparative Writing

Erica L. Johnson
Pace University
New York, NY, USA

Palgrave Studies in Affect Theory and Literary Criticism
ISBN 978-3-030-02097-2   ISBN 978-3-030-02098-9   (eBook)
https://doi.org/10.1007/978-3-030-02098-9

Library of Congress Control Number: 2018957686

This Palgrave Pivot imprint is published by the registered company Springer Nature
Switzerland AG
The registered company address is: Gewerbestrasse 11, 6330 Cham, Switzerland

ACKNOWLEDGEMENTS

Writing this book has for the most part been an exciting and satisfying process thanks to the inspiration and support I have received from so many. I am grateful to Pace University for a summer research grant that allowed me to do some key library work, and to Eugene Richie for stepping in to chair our department for a year while I finished the manuscript. I am deeply grateful to Rodolphe Hammadi for not only allowing me to publish his extraordinary photos, but for so quickly sending me excellent files of them. At Pace, I also want to thank Sid Ray, Catherine Zimmer, Sarah Blackwood, and Stephanie Hsu for their camaraderie and conversations about many of the topics I cover here. I am thankful to Ebele Oseye for sharing both insight and history with me. I wrote this book while working with the amazing Éloïse Brezault on our volume on cultural memory (*Memory as Colonial Capital*) and our related MLA panel, and I have learned so much from her. I would like to thank another member of that MLA panel, Marianne Hirsch, for her incredible generosity and her pioneering work, and for bringing me in to the Columbia University Cultural Memory Colloquium, another source of inspiration. Thanks to Steve Thomas for reading an early draft and talking through so much of this material along the way. Elaine Savory has been a wonderful source of support on this project and I also thank her for her photos of the Barbados monuments. I thank my cousin Kiran Obee for her genuine interest in this project and for a great monument tip. Jean Halley, whose work is one of my subjects here, is always an inspiration and I am grateful to her and to Patricia Moynagh for their support and friendship. Thanks too to Wendy Nielsen for her friendship and for sending me the cfp that kicked off this entire project, and thanks to Patricia Moran for her unconditional support of my work. I am grateful to my family and as always to Patrick and Max Johnson for our daily lives together.

Praise for *Cultural Memory, Memorials, and Reparative Writing*

"Interdisciplinary and international in scope; enviably concise in surveying, and astute in selecting and deploying, a wide range of scholarship; nuanced in demonstrating a reparative reading practice across different modalities; and elegantly persuasive in arguing 'the affective archive' *as method*, Professor Johnson's book makes productive reading for anyone interested in coming to terms, through cultural and memorial practices, with the afterlives of slavery."
—Donna Palmateer Pennee, *Western University, Canada*

CONTENTS

LIST OF FIGURES

CHAPTER 1

A Brief Introduction

Abstract This introduction lays out the three distinct areas that the book covers in its discussion of the uses of memory and affective material as sources of knowledge. These three areas include: critical theory, memoir, and memorials. The introduction begins with the topic of public memorials having to do with the racial history of the United States, and acknowledges the urgency of this topic in the wake of the Confederate monument removals and clashes in 2017 and ongoing debates about them. It ties these public debates about cultural memory to forms of writing that draw on personal forms of memory to do critical and cultural memory work.

Keywords Memorials · Memoir · Race · Affect theory · Cultural memory

The point of origin for *Cultural Memory, Memorials, and Reparative Writing* was my interest in the increasingly experimental writing of affect theorists who were shifting into a more personal and subjective idiom than is typical of academic prose. Not only were writers in the field pushing the boundaries of humanistic and social science research methods with these stylistic innovations, but they were introducing a new form of source material through their use of their own feelings and memories as evidence for their studies. Starting with an analysis of how personal

E. L. Johnson, *Cultural Memory, Memorials, and Reparative Writing*, Palgrave Studies in Affect Theory and Literary Criticism, https://doi.org/10.1007/978-3-030-02098-9_1

memory has come to form an important affective layer in scholarship, I connect the use of memory in writing with the rise of cultural memory studies, thereby moving from personal to collective uses of memory as a basis of research and a source of knowledge. Whereas the first two chapters of this short book present readings of how individual writers employ memory in theoretical texts and memoirs, the last chapter addresses cultural memory as it plays out on the emotional stage of public memorials and monuments. Memory—personal and cultural—has come to form an important archival source in how we write about, and feel about, culture and history.

That last chapter, on monuments and memorials, took on urgency in the summer of 2017. My focus is on the dearth of American memorial markers to the history of slavery, and in the course of doing that research I learned of the hundreds of Confederate monuments that pockmark the United States. Doing this research in 2015 and 2016, I was stunned by the indifferent or even defensive stances that city councils and state and federal congressional bodies held toward these symbols of oppression. Several states even passed legislation as recently as 2015 and 2016 that prevented or made difficult the removal of Confederate monuments, largely in response to the removal of the Confederate flag from the South Carolina capitol grounds at the late date of 2015. Other Confederate monuments have even gone up in the twenty-first century. These statues have always had their protesters, but before 2017 they stood for the most part undisturbed and unquestioned. People still walk by them every day on their way to work; public parks and government buildings sport these tributes to division and white supremacy; national and local holidays play out in their shadows in parks across the country. However, in May of 2017, Mayor Mitch Landrieu of New Orleans removed four monuments, three of which featured Confederate generals and one of which commemorated a race riot. As I write, such monuments are being acknowledged, questioned, and in more and more cases, removed. They have also become lightning rods for national feelings: likenesses of Robert E. Lee and Jefferson Davis—once overlooked or tolerated as though they were just part of the woodwork—are now sites of anger, despair, and frustration for most, and they are sites of pride and hatred for the white nationalist fringe. This was painfully borne out by the deadly clash between hate groups and counterprotesters in Charlottesville in August of 2017 that had its roots in a conflict over whether to remove a Lee monument. And so far the conversation around monument removal has entirely to do with what they *do* represent, namely white supremacy, and whether they have any value as reminders of an ugly history. What has not been explored is that the removal of the monuments will do nothing to make the history of the oppressed more visible; what has not been said is that there are so few monuments to black history in the first place that the Confederate monuments amount to double erasure. Taking down the statues does not result in gaps or absences in the material landscape of history insofar as those gaps and absences already exist. The country is already barren of markers to its Native American, Mexican, and African American histories to cite just some of the voids.

And why are memorials important? Aren't multiple histories remembered in art, literature, and academic work? Books can and do testify, and certainly poets and novelists have led the charge into the past in works from Toni Morrison's *Beloved* and Octavia Butler's *Kindred* to Claudia Rankine's *Citizen: An American Lyric* and Colson Whitehead's *Underground Railroad*. Along with these and many other literary memorials—for such is their status—memorial sites in public space are sites of memory where history and memory converge; where memory becomes history and history becomes memory through the feelings that memorials inspire in their viewers. As the flaring passions surrounding monuments in 2017 demonstrate, public art flows in and out of our personal identities.

Moreover, the feelings that monuments inspire in viewers reflect the shape of the viewer's knowledge (or ignorance) about the past. I therefore lead up to my analysis of memorials through a presentation of writing that incorporates memory traces as forms of affective knowledge. The first chapter, "In Theory: Memory as an Affective Archive," situates the book in the field of affect studies. I take as my starting point the "affective turn" that twenty-first-century criticism has taken and the transdisciplinary cohort of social scientists and humanists that has formed around methodologies that incorporate feelings and physiology into intellectual inquiry. These writers build on the tradition of observation, analysis, and archival research in the course of forging new critical pathways through the lived, phenomenological experiences of reflection and memory; they also build on the work of Audre Lorde, bell hooks, Minnie Bruce Pratt, Gloria Anzaldùa, and the many feminists who centralized bodies, feelings, and personal experience in their theoretical writing. Affect theorists have forged a new research methodology that extends from the use of emotional and embodied experience in theorizing social life, to the uses of memory as an archival source. To cite one example, Ann Cvetkovich demonstrates this method in her recent *An Archive of Feelings* and in a text I discuss at length, *Depression: A Public Feeling*. In the latter book, Cvetkovich draws on "academic memoir" by embedding her own "Depression Journals" in her scholarly critique of the medicalization of depression. I look at this and other examples of academic memoir and journaling as scholarly sources in contemporary affect theory.

In Chapter 2, "Memoir and Memory-traces" I turn to memoir work that, like the work of affect theorists, engages the archive through affect. The "archive" is an admittedly profuse concept and it means different things in different contexts. In an academic context, archival materials include most recorded and retrievable sources which, traditionally, have served as the basis for substantiating scholarship. As Derrida notes in *Archive Fever*, though, "the archive takes place at the place of originary and structural breakdown of the said memory" (Derrida 11). The archive is thus entangled with memory by definition, as it poses as an externalized, disembodied form of cultural memory that the scholar can mine. As a property of memory, so too is the archive a property of history, and it is this form of archive that Caribbean writers Dionne Brand and Patrick Chamoiseau engage in works that span memoir and history. Brand's memoir, *A Map to the Door of No Return: Notes to Belonging*, touches on the author's childhood in Trinidad and adulthood in Canada but is equally concerned with understanding and intervening in the larger histories amongst which Brand situates her identity. A lush work of memories, poetry, and criticism, the book presents vignettes from the author's life alongside her meditations on writing, history, mapmaking, and most importantly for this chapter, the archives. Brand's memoir is replete with supporting materials that range from fifteenth-century journals and letters to contemporary critical theory, from geographers' logs to films and pop culture. While her sources are rich and varied, they can be broken down into three general types: there are the historical archives written during the "age of exploration" and the slave trade; the contemporary archives of newspapers and journals; and the creative archive of postcolonial literature, or what I have elsewhere termed the neo-archive.[1] Brand's memoir participates in an entire genre of postcolonial writing that enters and intervenes in the colonial archive through memories and feelings.

While Brand engages with literal and literary archival sources and puts them into dialogue with her own memoir work, Patrick Chamoiseau theorizes memory in his remarkable account of French Guiana's history as a penal colony in *Guyane: Traces-mémoires du bagne* [French Guiana: Memory-traces of the Penal Colony], in which he does memory work similar to that of Brand by creating an affective archive of the feelings he experienced as he explored the ruins of the prisons with the photographer Rodolphe Hammadi. Like Brand's memoir, Chamoiseau's work is constructed of poetic fragments that combine the recorded history of French Guiana with the hauntings that it provokes in the author. *Guyane* thus presents a neo-archive of photographs and feelings that present history through an affective lens.

Finally, in the third chapter entitled "Memory, Affect, and Countermonuments," I turn to monuments and memorials. No longer limited by embodiment, or what Marianne Hirsch refers to as "indexical memory," memory exceeds the liberal subject and becomes a collective practice in cultural sites like monuments. I look at the problem of memorializing traumatic histories and monumental practices in the United States and the Caribbean with regard to the African diasporic histories that knit the region together. I then turn my attention to a case study of monumental art by Kara Walker, an artist who demonstrates as clearly as anyone that public art is controversial precisely because it provokes powerful feelings of shame, wonder, disgust, sublimity, anger, and humility in her viewers. I focus on Walker's colossal sugar sculpture entitled "A Subtlety, or the Marvelous Sugar Baby," which loomed over thousands of viewers from around the world in the ruins of a sugar factory in Brooklyn during the summer of 2014. I argue that Walker's piece constitutes what Robert Young and Richard Crownshaw have defined as "countermonumental" art, and I contextualize it in the fraught and partial material record of monuments to black history in the Americas. The figure of a caricatured black woman posed in the crouch of ancient allusion, the sculpture was made of 40,000 tons of sugar and has been referred to as both a stately "sphinx" and a deeply offensive "mammy." *A Subtlety* embodied the repressed histories of the sugar industry in a stunning materiality all the more haunting for its dissolution back into immateriality. A figure of the Americas and a controversial memorial to the violence and coerced labor upon which sugar plantations and refineries relied, Walker's sculpture and the "molasses boys" who surrounded her erupted from the hauntings of history and reside now only in the archive of cultural memory and, for those who visited, in the remembered feelings, smells, and sounds of the ruined factory. Arguably a *lieu de mémoire*, or a site where memory and history converge (Pierre Nora), the statue is also a *Traces-mémoires* (Chamoiseau) in the sense that, unlike most monuments, her form dissolved and she leaves only affective traces.[2]

Moreover, her absence mimetically represents the absence in the United States of memorials to the millions of enslaved people who toiled on its shores for centuries. In contrast to most Caribbean countries, which feature memorials that commemorate the lives of enslaved people as well as monuments to Maroon heroes and to emancipation, the United States has few such markers. The absence of such a memorial in the nation's capital, and the fact that the single federally funded memorial to the enslaved was erected as recently as 2010 in Philadelphia, speaks to the willful amnesia of the present and the silenced, if haunting, archives of the past. Walker's countermonument supplements existing archives and material traces with affective knowledge through her powerfully controversial figure, and at the same time *A Subtlety's* ghostliness embodies the absent memorials of this country. As Young says in *The Texture of Memory*, in phrasing that mimes the paradox of memorializing trauma, "How does one represent an absence? In this case, by representing it" (Young 45).

By examining the ways in which memory has been integrated into archival engagement in the three distinct areas of critical theory, memoir, and memorial art, *Cultural Memory, Memorials, and Reparative Writing* contributes to recent work in affect studies and cultural memory studies. Memory as method; memory as archive; memorial as affect: the book looks at the interplay between archival research and archival sources on the one hand, and the affective memories, both personal and collective, that flow from, around, and into the constantly shifting record of social phenomena and history.

NOTES

1. Some of this description of Brand's book is taken from my article, "Building the Neo-Archive: Dionne Brand's *A Map to the Door of No Return.*" *Meridians* 12.1 (2014): 149–171.
2. Chamoiseau always uses his term "Traces-mémoires" in the plural, even when grammar would indicate a singular usage.

CHAPTER 2

In Theory:
Memory as an Affective Archive

Abstract This chapter focuses on methodology in the field of affect studies. The discussion focuses on three contemporary studies of affective epistemology and traces this epistemology back to its intellectual foremothers in addition to linking it to Eve Sedgwick's notion of "reparative reading." The three case studies that exemplify what I call "reparative writing" include Jean Halley's *The Parallel Lives of Women and Cows: Meat Markets*, Anne Cvetkovich's *Depression: A Public Feeling*, and Elspeth Probyn's *Blush: Faces of Shame*. Each author draws on personal memories as crucial sources of material in much the same way that they draw on more standard archival materials, thereby demonstrating their use of an "affective archive."

Keywords Reparative writing · Journal · Memoir · Depression · Trauma · Shame

A distinguishing feature of twenty-first-century criticism is that it has taken an "affective turn," and although the term has gained considerable traction in the past decade, it is not to be taken for granted. Indeed, this shift is among the most consequential when one considers that the academic discourse of objective observation, scientific method, and purely rational investigation has dominated intellectual inquiry for centuries. So closely have literary and cultural criticism hewn to these methodologies

© The Author(s) 2018   7
E. L. Johnson, *Cultural Memory, Memorials, and Reparative Writing*, Palgrave Studies in Affect Theory and Literary Criticism, https://doi.org/10.1007/978-3-030-02098-9_2

that the few writers who have begun to explore the role of feelings, emotions, and physical sensations in both their subjects of study and those who study them, have begun to form a distinct transdisciplinary critical presence.[1] In many ways, affect theory is indebted to feminist theory with its earlier critiques of epistemic systems that reproduced what psychoanalysts identified as normatively male object relations and ways of knowing, and it has developed in tandem with queer theory that seeks to recoup a past of long hidden desires and feelings. Feminism and queer theory very much influence the works that I will address here, works by literary and cultural critics Ann Cvetkovich and Elspeth Probyn and by sociologist Jean O'Malley Halley. These exemplars of affective methodology are pioneers of affect theory in their own right and yet they build on the tradition of observation, analysis, and archival research in the course of forging new critical pathways through the lived, phenomenological experiences of reflection and memory. More specifically, these writers provide the most prominent examples of a new research methodology that rests on a concept of not only feelings, but of affective memory as an archival source, as Cvetkovich demonstrates in her recent *An Archive of Feelings* and as she explains elsewhere: "exemplifying deconstructive principles, academic memoir can expose the material conditions and subject positions that underlie intellectual production" (Cvetkovich 75). And, as Halley argues, memory is a site of the social. In keeping with Hirsch's demonstration that memory is not locked into individual experience but that it circulates through individuals through forces of history and culture, Halley's sociological approach to her own memories reveals their larger cultural implications.

This turn toward the affective archive as a research method is at least in part a response to the failure of more objective methods to reveal the workings of power and meaning on the most intimate, and hence forceful, level. In a sense, it has long been the goal of feminist and cultural criticism to reveal and thus challenge normalized structures of gender, race, sexuality, and so forth, yet how are we to really see daily, lived experience through intellectual inquiry alone? Theoretical, literary, and cultural texts are indeed rich sources of material, as are archival sources, and such texts have long formed the basis of study. However, as the writers I will explore in this chapter demonstrate, such textual sources can be engaged through personal and emotional, as well as intellectual, points of entry. This direction has been mapped out to date by scholars of queer studies who make the case for drawing on queer lived experience and creative expression as part of the critical enterprise. Cvetkovich makes such an argument in *An Archive of Feelings* and Heather Love, in *Feeling Backward*, reads queer texts of modernism as "a crucial 'archive of feeling,' an account of the corporeal and psychic costs of homophobia" (Love 4). These writers turn to affect as a mode of entering the archive because, to really understand the workings of power and the embodied experience of history and culture, they turn inward as well as outward and in so doing they have developed a means of discerning that which has been normalized. Thus, feeling backward, and exploring archives of feeling, are methods that critically draw together intensely personal and intimate experience with larger social and historical meanings. And since the intimate corollary to history is memory, these writers plumb the depths of personal and cultural memory in order to expand the reach of academic method.

What I would like to suggest here is that the use of memory as a source, as an affective archive in the experimental writing and in the art that I explore in this book, offers an important corollary to Eve Kosofsky Sedgwick's notion of "reparative" reading. Drawing on Melanie Klein's notion of the various "positions" through which we form subjectivity, Sedgwick explains that the vast majority of critical work stems from a "paranoid" position. She explains that "'hermeneutics of suspicion'—widespread critical habits indeed, [are] perhaps by now nearly synonymous with criticism itself—may have had an unintentionally stultifying side effect: they may have made it less rather than more possible to unpack the local, contingent relations between any given piece of knowledge and its narrative/epistemological entailments for the seeker, knower, or teller" (Sedgwick 124). As Love interprets Sedgwick, "paranoid reading is described as a way of disavowing affect in order to claim ownership over truth" (Love 237). In a break from "paranoid" criticism, a reparative reading strategy relinquishes "the knowing, anxious paranoid determination that no horror, however apparently unthinkable, shall ever come to the reader as *new*" (Sedgwick 146).[2] Whereas (paranoid) critical reading has long played out as a process of debunking, or of revealing underlying and insidious ideological structures, a reparative reader approaches texts with an openness to what it conveys about not only epistemes, but about human experience in its plenitude. I argue that writers who draw upon their affective archives in pursuit of scholarly endeavor do reparative writing. Just as reparative reading is open to a text's emotional as well as intellectual layers, reparative writing opens up intellectual inquiry to material that has long been hidden in the shadow of method. As historian Joan Scott says in her discussion of "the evidence of experience," writers who draw on experience can "document the experience of those institutions in all their variety and multiplicity, to write about and thus render historical what has hitherto been hidden from history" (Scott 80). And, crucially, this means opening oneself to past feelings without a filter, political or psychological. This is why Love looks at fictions of queer modernity that describe "living with injury—not fixing it" (Love 4). Whereas critical work is often tasked with reclaiming or improving upon painful histories, reparative writing is more flatly mimetic and less judgmental or even interpretive. The texts I will examine all present painful pasts, and whereas representation *is* resistance to some extent, their openness to "negative" affects is key to the reparative work they do.

No longer constrained to established methodologies or to preexisting archives, then, writers and artists expand upon conventional academic resources to include the affective archives of long marginalized feelings and memories as rich sites of social meaning and as crucial lenses through which to view the world. This is also evident in the new and growing field of cultural memory studies, which recognizes the utility of memory as a research method. Astrid Erll and Ann Regney explain that "the very concept of *cultural* memory is itself premised on the idea that memory can only become collective as a part of a continuous process whereby memories are shared with the help of symbolic artifacts that mediate between individuals and, in the process, create communality across both space and time" (Erll and Regney 1). The hinge of memory thus conjoins the intimate with the public in both contemporary work and in queer and feminist writing that preceded it.

For example, at the 2015 "Affect Theory Conference: Worldings/ Tensions/ Futures," perhaps no writer was more prominently mentioned than Audre Lorde. Scholars from a myriad of disciplines drew on and performed close readings of Lorde's writing from her *Cancer Journals*, which model the fusion of personal memory and reflection with academic investigation, to her now-canonical essays. Lorde argued that the source of critical power lies not only within the mind, but within the body and the feelings that the world inspires within us. For example, her essay entitled "Uses of Anger: Women Responding to Racism" takes the feeling of anger as a starting point and, in the course of her investigation of its pitfalls and uses, she examines as well the toxic axis of anger and fear, as well as that of guilt—of which she remarks, "I have no creative use for guilt, yours or my own" (Lorde 130). Lorde's affective interface with the politics of black queer feminist thought lays the groundwork for twenty-first-century analyses of "affective labor," as we see in such recent work as Shiloh Whitney's essay about "Affective Indigestion: Lorde, Fanon, and Gutierrez-Rodriguez on Race and Affective Labor," which draws on Lorde's differentiation between "digestible" and "indigestible" anger. Lorde's bodily metaphors, such as digesting anger and metaboliz-ing racism, operate powerfully at the affective intersection of mind, body, and feelings, and thus her theorizing of affect maps out the burgeon-ing methodology of a field that did not yet exist while Lorde was writ-ing; what is more, her *affective writing* anticipates twenty-first-century methodology.

One element of Lorde's affective writing is her use of memory, which she employs as evidence of the ideas she theorizes. In another essay on anger, "Eye to Eye: Black Women, Hatred, and Anger," she presents her memory of visiting a racist optometrist when she was three, a racist librarian when she was six, a racist waiter in her adolescence, and another racist and sexually predatory optometrist in her young adulthood. While her topic remains the silt layers of anger that accumulate into "a fen of unexplained anger that encircled me... a pool of acid deep inside me, and whenever I felt deeply, I felt it, attaching itself in the strangest places" (Lorde 150), this topic rests on the evidence of her own mem-ories. Employing memory as academic and political evidence, Lorde eschews the value of objectivity even as she embraces that of research in her investigation of racialized subjectivity in the United States. Hence, it is not just that she writes from deep within her own subjectivity, but her arrangement of that subjectivity through memory and through feeling, that makes her work a rhetorical as well as philosophical scaffolding for affect theorists.

I would point to bell hooks and Gloria Anzaldúa as other promi-nent foremothers of contemporary discourse, with hooks's power-ful first-person voice in her many volumes and of course Anzaldúa's highly poetic and personal voice in *Borderlands/La Frontera*, in which she recalls dreams and memories alike in order to express the complex-ity of her ethnic and sexual identities. Recounting the memory of a spiritual encounter with a red snake, she reflects, "We're not supposed to remember such otherworldly events. We're supposed to ignore, for-get, kill those fleeting images of the soul's presence and of the spirit's presence" (Anzaldúa 36). She explains that this amnesia is meant in particular to maintain the body–mind binary against which Sedgwick argues. Thus these twentieth-century feminist writers present earlier examples of reparative writing that incorporates mind, body, and feelings into analyses of oppression and celebrations of intersectional identities alike.

My emphasis, then, is on both the trove of material available in textual and archival sources, and material that resides within the reader, writer, and subject of study. The concept of the archive is endlessly useful when approached through affect theory—but why the archive? Archives are increasingly important to postcolonial, feminist, and queer studies as well as other related fields because, as Kate Eichhorn explains in *The Archival Turn in Feminism*, the archive is "not a place to discover the past but rather a way to engage with some of the legacies, epistemes, and traumas pressing down on the present" (Eichhorn 5). Eichhorn's emphasis on trauma, alongside the broader terms of legacies and epistemes, speaks to the status of the archive as a collection of that which is recorded, and that which cannot be—as a record of absence, too. That is, trauma is demonstrably extratextual; it haunts narrative but does not enter into it. The impact of trauma on the archive is that it renders it porous; it imputes the failure to save, transcribe, and remember. For example, Marilyn Booth, in writing about how nineteenth-century-Arab women turned to fiction as a means of presenting material refused by the "official" archive, makes the helpful observation that, "if 'archive' suggests a fixity, a fixing of boundaries around what counts as history," then the novel she discusses presents an "archive that is of the absences in the available historical narratives… as they have been remembered in national histories" (Booth 287). The archive, in all of its exclusions and failures, remains an important point of reference for those who circumvent and challenge it through fiction, memoir, and other creative forms of interface. As I have argued elsewhere, an entire genre of postcolonial historical fiction, which I refer to as "ghostwriting," has emerged from the hauntings of archives that are not only incomplete, but violently so.[3] Similarly, Randy Bass goes so far as to say that "knowledge making depends on the creative straining of the story against the archive. That's where meaning lives" (in Booth 292). This is certainly the basis of the texts I will examine here, for they establish a shared methodology across disciplines and topics that are born of the friction between the public archive of textuality, and the private archives of memory.

Prominently inspired by Foucault, scholars of affect who work in the social sciences and humanities adapt his practice of scouring the archive for evidence of social meaning and change by incorporating into such work their own personal archival material including memoir, diaries, and memory poems. To wit, sociologists Grace Cho and Jackie Orr have written scholarly books that are openly based upon and shaped by such personal experiences as immigration and diaspora, and panic disorder, respectively, while Patricia Ticinto Clough has incorporated memory poems into her work on the changing nature of our relationships to technology. Similarly, Lauren Berlant, Kathleen Stewart, and others have written about literary and cultural phenomena from deeply personal experience. In a related vein, Ann Laura Stoler has presented, in a more conventionally academic voice, the helpful concept of the "intimate archive" by combing through colonial archives for evidence of the feelings that bound colonial subjects to one another within and across the conceptual binary of colonizer/colonized, and she has explored the network of feelings among families and within domestic situations in such a way that they cannot be reduced to overdetermined social and political structures of power.[4] This is to say that Halley, Probyn, and Cvetkovich are in good company, and that they are working in a burgeoning field of study by approaching both affect and the archive through their reparative writing.

To map out this chapter: I will discuss Halley's sociological analysis of the US beef industry, presented through the lens of trauma memoir, along with Ann Cvetkovich's *Depression: A Public Feeling*, in which she inserts her own "depression journals" into a critique of the medicalization of depression, and Elspeth Probyn's *Blush: Faces of Shame*, in which she draws on personal memories in order to gracefully underscore her somewhat controversial presentation of the shame affect. Each of these writers regards memory as source material that exceeds individual experience; they draw on their feelings and experiences as signifiers of culturally normative practices and values—and thus locate memory on a continuum that extends from the individual body that houses memory to posthuman networks of meaning. In so doing, they reveal even the most normalized flows of power. Rather than observing that there is a floor under our feet, for example, we might see "the grit… [that] fills in the cracks, the gaps, the empty spaces in the floor... life's leavings" (Halley 1); we might see "the tiny cracks in glass that surround the small hole made by a bullet. The hole itself is empty, clear open space. The cracks simply, gently mark the glass, remaining in it, of it and distinct, all at once" (Halley 5).

Such is the vision of Halley.[5] In poetic voice and through humbling narratives, she splices together the quotidian violence of the meat industry with the trauma of growing up on a cattle ranch amidst cruelty that ensnared humans and animals alike. In her book *The Parallel Lives of Women and Cows: Meat Markets*, Halley presents a meticulously researched history of the origins and development of the American beef industry in dialogue with her childhood memories. If Upton Sinclair famously "aimed for the public's heart, and by accident... hit it in the stomach" (Halley 130) with *The Jungle*, Halley's work continues the tradition of powerful exposé while achieving his original goal of moving her readers on an emotional level. She does this by interspersing archival research about beef, the Irish famine and subsequent waves of emigration that sent her ancestors across the Atlantic, and the conquest of what is now the western United States with the affective archives of her own memories. And, because the memories she explores are those of trauma, the entire book is shaped as a trauma narrative, shaped by the violence Halley experienced as a girl and that with which she and her abusers were surrounded on the cattle ranch where she grew up. Like the memories, which loop and repeat around barely representable experiences of sexual abuse and exposure to cruelty, the story of cattle becoming capital circles back on itself to fold in such layers as migration, race, conquest, and dehumanization. From the outset, Halley combines theoretical and personal material by explaining that, "as many people who write about trauma or work with traumatized subjects note, trauma often grips the survivor in waves of repetitive experience," and "I also repeat scenes, and in particular one scene involving my sister and me, again and again" (Halley 5). The result is an almost incantatory prose, as gripping of the reader as the stories it tells were of its writer.

Halley's experimental writing charts a new course for study of the social that reads and represents affective experience. Memory is a particularly important affective archive in the sense that, given the vast trove of individual memories we each have, and the even greater gaps between them, writing memories into evidence is an act of self-archiving that, when incorporated into more traditional research, provides key details and nuances of underlying social meaning. In her articulation of the paradoxical task of representing that which has been normalized, Halley puts it thus: "even at a cellular level in my family, we became gendered and sexual beings through violence. It was like water to a fish, so close we could not see it, know it, realize it, speak it" (Halley 17). There is no external record of this state of being, no psychologist's notes or witness accounts on which to draw. There is, however, an internal, psychic record, and this is what Halley records in her book.

Halley frames her self-portrait of "girl-consciousness" with an analysis of the beef industry, in part because it is the context of her childhood and in part because it forms a backdrop to American history and identity. As Teresa Brennan notes in *The Transmission of Affect*, "affects have an energetic dimension... we are not self-contained in terms of our energies. There is no secure distinction between 'the individual' and 'the environment'" (Brennan 6). In light of the affective flow that binds individuals to their environments, Halley's description of the beef industry hovers over that of violence in the home. She goes into the details of just what mass industrial farming involves, from its sheer scale (130,000 cattle and 7000 calves are slaughtered every day in the United States) to its effects on the lives of beef cows and on the people who work in slaughterhouses. Not only are cows killed en masse—sometimes while conscious—but their lifespan and physiology have also been altered so that most beef cows now live for fourteen to sixteen months in a state of extreme obesity caused by industrial feed. The human dimension of this process includes placing workers in harm's way both emotionally and physically. Many spend their days stunning, "shackling," and slicing up cows' bodies hour after hour, an exposure to violence that finds its way into the family and community life as well. Halley cites studies that demonstrate increased crime rates and rates of domestic abuse in communities with high slaughterhouse employment, which "suggest that the increase in family violence indicates 'a connection between the victimization of animals and the victimization of less powerful human groups, such as children and women'" (Halley 135).[6] As Halley demonstrates, beef production and consumption is practiced in such a way that it sends shivers of violence out into the world yet remains a socially acceptable act; in fact, when pressed to identify an "American" cuisine, many will point to the hamburger, or to steak—which is to say that eating beef is somehow integral to national identity.

As a companion narrative to her memories, then, the story of beef bears national scars, for she explains how the conversion of beef into not only a mass market food product, but into capital, is the essence of the American beef story. Halley's history and assessment of the beef industry touches on every aspect of it from the fearful efficiencies of slaughter and meatpacking that have landed beef at the center of the American diet to the ripple effect that cow consumption has had on agriculture more broadly. This history bears on Halley's life not only because she is an American, but more specifically "there is a shared history between my family and American beef cows. Fundamentally, both are stories of violence" (Halley 11). The "parallel lives" that Halley describes, between women and cows, are similar in that both are predicated on forms of masculinity as an aggressive, invasive force. That said, the personal connection she traces between the beef industry and familial violence reflect back on larger social structures of gender and power, and therefore "[b]oth the story of U.S. beef and my childhood illuminate the defining and disciplining of contemporary life" (Halley 16). The scholarly and affective archives upon which she draws thus underscore her sociological investigation in equal measure.

Although there are demonstrable parallels between the violence of the industry and that which Halley experienced as a child, it is her reparative writing, her affective methodology, that defines her argument. Scott notes the critical confluence of "public" and "private" writing in her observation that "although one seems to be about society, the public and the political, and the other is about the individual, the private, and the psychological, in fact both narratives are inescapably historical; they are discursive productions of knowledge of the self, not reflections either of external or internal truth" (Scott 94). Halley draws upon both writerly positions, and if her prose is compelling when she writes about the history of beef, it is visceral in the passages of memory in which she comes to grips with the violence through which "girl-consciousness" is produced. She presents her memory work through reparative writing in the sense that she refuses to foreclose such stigmatized feelings as terror or shame; just as reparative reading is open to the fullness of a text by holding off on diagnosing or pathologizing the problems it presents, reparative writing records even profound problems as such, in a raw and uncodified state. Halley presents a historical narrative whereby westward expansion in the United States was propelled by cattle and conquest and, at a fundamental level, by a penetrating masculinity that also invaded the bodies of girls and women in the home. She provides evidence for this through her discursive reading of the history of American conquest, and by delving into her memories of her father and grandfather. She notes the overwhelming presence of violence in her family when she says of her mother, "she came from brutality and married it. Like all of us tumbling through time, in motion, and held tightly, all at once" (Halley 53). She observes of her grandfather Clarke that "Clarke, Clarke it seemed to me was simply cruel. Clarke was cruelty out of nowhere… And everyone pretended everything was okay. Everyone pretended not to see. Or maybe, maybe, they were not pretending. Maybe if one does not see for so long, too long, generations, one loses the capacity to see. Or maybe blindness simply ran in the family. I don't know" (Halley 82). In these passages, Halley demonstrates the process of normalization within her family as a hallmark of similar processes such as gender becoming manifest through acts of male violence on female bodies. So when Clarke and his son enact violence and violation on the most vulnerable members of the family, little girls, these acts are socially freighted even as they are acts of cruel individuals.

Halley makes this confluence terrifyingly clear in a recurrent memory to which she refers in her opening, the memory involving her sister. The memory, which surfaces throughout the book in the cyclical pattern of trauma, is of her father forcing his two very young daughters to stand in a cold garage in the middle of the night while he takes her sister's beloved cat, "all black, soft and sleek," and slaughters it, telling the girls: "I am a man" (Halley 24). The gutted cat reappears in the course of Halley's narrative of beef, linking as it does the site of trauma with that of masculinity, and the act of slaughter that is normalized on a cattle ranch with deeply intimate harm in the home. This primal scene lays bare the effects of normalized violence whether against humans or animals—it invokes the effects of slaughter on human workers who enact gutting day after day in repetitions powered by the conversion of cattle into capital. As Norman K. Denzin notes in his reading of this scene, the father's declaration, "I am a man," means "[I am] a man who kills animals" (Denzin 5). His gendered identity is predicated on violence, on slaughter. After a repetition of the memory, Halley writes, "Real men could never be submissive, never be entered, but only actively move forward, entering others, entering the conquered" (Halley 27), and the intimate corollary to the history of national conquest is the inscription of "real" masculinity on the bodies of girls and women within the realm of the family. This is not to say that Halley suggests a purely causal relationship between violence against animals and sexual violence, although in her own experience the two are implicated in one another. Through her titular concept of parallel lives, Halley allows readers to see violence toward animals and girls as sometimes causal, sometimes mutually reflective, and sometimes coextensive. The link between the two, though, remains a gender narrative whereby "being a man meant rupturing the other, bursting through barriers of skin and flesh in violence, all too often sexual. To some extent I think this reflected manhood in the larger normative cultures" (Halley 88). The same men in her story who tear apart the bodies of cats and cows, violate the bodies of little girls. Hence in her chapter about "The Production of Girl Life and the Lives of Girls," Halley shows how the encryption of violence into American masculinity works to normalize "girl-experience" as a state of "no-longer-being-embodied. Instead my form became the surface for the pleasure of another" (Halley 81).

Moreover, Halley argues that this particular form of masculinity is uniquely American, and she makes her point by historicizing the development of her family's American identity upon arriving from Ireland in the nineteenth century. The co-author of *Seeing White: An Introduction to White Privilege and Race*, Halley is ever attentive to the role that race plays in any American family and story. Extrapolating from the racial politics of colonial Ireland, where her Catholic ancestors were subjected to inhuman treatment and discriminatory laws by the Protestant and English power structure, Halley traces the ugly evolution of that identity on contact with the United States. The morphing of "Irish" identity into American whiteness is itself a tale of social violence and one that Halley folds into her portrait of her childhood. She explains how, "In the United States, the new Irish Catholic immigrants stepped quickly into the role of the Protestants in Ireland. And like the Protestants in Ireland, Irish Catholic Americans might be living miserable, poverty-stricken lives, yet they could always soothe themselves with their newfound privilege of whiteness" (Halley 45). Whereas economic solidarity with African Americans, in particular, might have improved the living and working conditions for multiple oppressed groups, Halley makes a point that resonates powerfully in this decade following the publication of her book when she says "the white working class in the United States chose greater psychic power instead of opting for the potential power of greater numbers—bargaining power—had they organized together with the least powerful in their society" (Halley 46). Like other areas of her book that address national history through scholarly research, Halley substantiates her narrative of Irish American history with memories of her own family. She concludes the chapter on Irish immigration with a repetition of the cat memory, connecting that act of violence with her father's sense of himself as a *white* man; later in the book she reveals a nightmarish memory of her grandfather's participation in a grisly Ku Klux Klan ritual. She thus illustrates how the toxicity of race relations in the U.S. poisons her life even in all of its rural remoteness.

Another dimension of her method is that Halley presents a distinct formal approach to the inscription of family trauma within national violence. She does this by clearly delineating the voices in which she writes so that they tell two distinct narratives that play off of one another, and the most prominent way in which she does this is to record her memory passages in a different font than those that present her scholarly research. In so doing, she enacts the "creative straining of the story against the archive" that Bass says constitutes knowledge itself (in Booth 292). The sans serif, blocky font of the memories echo their rawness, as though the letters are as stripped down as the stories they tell, while the slightly more ornate serif script of the research flows around the harsh fragments. This stylistic choice also enables the reader to take in, at a glance, the path of each page as when, for example, a blocky scrap stands apart on the page: "And he took the cat. I am a man he told us" (Halley 29), and Halley goes on to observe in the other font, "Really, everyone is always transformed, always changed by their encounter with the edge of themselves. And when it comes to cows, they actually do change us as we encounter them. They are the animal edge, the frontier that we incorporate into us. We devour them and they transform our bodies anew. The cows quite literally become something more, something else. They become us" (Halley 29). By presenting her own story in free-standing passages upon which she makes relatively little commentary, Halley offers it as evidence alongside that of her scholarly research, evidence that the quotidian slaughter of animals functions as a bullet hole that sends slivers and shards of pain along the pane of the social—to invoke Halley's guiding metaphor of the fractures that surround the emptiness of a bullet hole.

The interlocking forms of manhood and "being-girl" that Halley describes have been explored, as she notes, by radical feminists dating back to the 1970s who understood violence to be "at the heart of gendered power" (Halley 88). Halley substantiates her own analysis of gender and power with a trauma memory that, symptomatically, exceeds language and representation. Trauma theorists Nicolas Abraham and Maria Torok refer to trauma as a "phantom" housed in a "crypt" of the psyche, and Cathy Caruth, whose work Halley invokes, argues that trauma is not "a possessed knowledge, but instead possesses, at will, the one it inhabits" (Caruth 6). Trauma makes for scant evidence. By drawing on her affective archive, though, Halley renders the haunting, unknowable content of trauma as such. While the scene with the cat repeats in the elliptical pattern of trauma flashbacks, she presents as well another traumatic memory that exceeds representation: "I remembered but I cannot take the memory out of my pocket. I remembered but I cannot show you the memory and say, see, here it is. I have nothing to show, only vagueness" (Halley 86). However, by harnessing the force of affect, she conveys through feeling what she cannot illustrate through evidence. Her construction of girl-being around silence, around that which is unspeakable and invisible, captures its traumatic essence. Moreover, the memory that does not exist is yet remembered, and the dissociation between the act of remembering and the material of memory serves as a crucial means of gaining leverage on trauma in Halley's memoir sections. Her clear claim that "I remember" enables her to establish agency in her narrative and to open with the claim that "this book is a story about being gripped by trauma and it is a story about finding some kind of freedom" (Halley 6), and to conclude it as a survivor for whom trauma "sometimes, pushes life forward" (Halley 160).

Indeed, recent work in cultural memory studies reconfigures memory in a way that alters our understanding of repression, trauma, and the function of screen memories. In his important book, *Multidirectional Memory*, Michael Rothberg expands upon psychoanalytic thought to suggest that "the displacement that takes place in screen memory (indeed, in all memory), functions as much to open up lines of communication with the past as to close them off" (Rothberg 12). Similarly, Max Silverman says of trauma that "subjects are not simply victims burdened with the melancholic repetition of a particular traumatic moment in the past but actively work through the interconnections between that moment and others" (Silverman 21). Through her ability to remember, her use of knowledge that resides in the body and in very real, representable feelings, Halley ultimately tells her story cathartically and as an activist enabling her readers to see long hidden, covert forms of violence enacted upon humans and animals alike. Like Halley, her readers "learn to see what had happened on the other side of the story we had called reality" (Halley 159).

Just as Halley's memory serves as a means of repairing the archive, as an intervention in the process of historical and national encodings of violence in the quotidian practices and intimate spaces of life, Cvetkovich faces off what she terms the "impasse" of critical discourse by offering her memories of depression as leverage on the liberal humanist understanding of depression as an individual pathology or as a personal failing. She describes her initial impetus to publish her memoirs as a response to the fact that she had read nothing about depression that either moved or haunted her. How can the literature on such a powerful feeling as depression be so clinical, so bereft of other feelings whether sympathetic or responsive—whether compassionate or deeply sad? Cvetkovich does a remarkable job of tracing the liberal formation of depression as an individual, medical ailment during the twentieth century, and in particular in the 1980s and 1990s, shaped as these decades were by Prozac and a revolution in antidepressants. In contrast to the recent medicalization and individualization of depression, she explains that its ancient antecedent, *acedia*, was understood among fourth-century monks to be a shared social condition of sadness rather than a treatable disease.

Like the concept of public feelings, Cvetkovich's use of personal journals, which she classifies as "academic memoir," supports the idea that memories, feelings, and experiences are not limited to the individual who lives them but rather that they signify and are signified by larger social moods and collective affects. The very idea of "public feelings" emerged from the "Feel Tank" gathering of scholars and activists who shared the view that feelings are as much social and political as they are personal in nature. The very reason that Cvetkovich and Halley draw on their memories as archival material is because they take a posthumanist approach to memory in which power, social relations, feelings, and knowledge flow through and around the medicalized body, in the case of depression, and the gendered body and animal body, in Halley's case. These bodies are coterminous with such forces as pharmaceuticals and violence that alter body, mind, and discourse. And both draw on affect because it offers a rare opportunity to, as Cvetkovich says, "circumvent the conscious mind in order to generate material from the places of feeling, including the body" (Cvetkovich 77). In other words, the affective archive exposes normalized values and phenomena that cannot be discerned through intellectual cognition. Halley's argument that such phenomena are "like water to a fish" applies to Cvetkovich's work in that, although depression is, in terms of social parlance and norms, a medicalized and pathologized negative feeling, she suggests that this view is water to fish who breathe in such assumptions. Sadness, melancholia, political despair—these feelings cannot be medicated away when they stem from systemic racism, economic oppression, gender injustice, and the many other flows of power and feeling that provoke what is usually called depression but what might, as Cvetkovich says, be "ordinary feelings embedded in ordinary circumstances" (Cvetkovich 79). As a research method, memoir breaks from pre-scripted models of identity to "track the life of the sensate being in the world," to see, for example, "*how capitalism feels* or *how diaspora feels*" (Cvetkovich 81).

Moreover, Cvetkovich develops her investigative method through her own brand of reparative writing in that she seeks to open academic work to a kind of "productivity" that defies political, social, and economic categories of value. She argues that academics are ensnared in a neoliberal condition of production whereby we are told to *produce* on the one hand, and told that our products have no real (i.e. monetary) value on the other hand, and she cautions that the miasma of the academy is then the feeling that "your work does not matter [which] is to feel dead inside, a condition that is normalized for so many [academics]" (Cvetkovich 18). Not only does this observation point to one of the many ways in which depression can be understood to be a public feeling—in this case, within the particular social context of academia—but Cvetkovich substantiates her argument through the evidence she provides in the form of a memory: she remembers her dissertation defense as abysmal, not because she failed to provide adequate explanations to her readers, but because, "as we discussed my work, I couldn't feel any sense of connection to it, couldn't claim it as my own to defend or celebrate" (Cvetkovich 33). A trigger of her own spiral into depression, this paradox between the rarified nature of scholarship and notions of value and productivity predicated on capital can indeed be damaging. Jani Scandura nails Cvetkovich's description of this conundrum when she comments, "To be an academic in the current corporate university, one must keep at it despite the overarching fear, and at times certainty, that academic labor and particularly humanistic labor, is time spent without value" (Scandura 159). While there is admittedly a degree of self-absorption in this discussion about academics by academics, both Cvetkovich and Scandura point to the neoliberal university as a contextual, public structure for academics' feelings of depression or anxiety. In response to this institutionally generated "public feeling" of worthlessness, Cvetkovich does reparative work by theorizing a notion of productivity and value of scholarship that lies not only in its scholarly or social impact, but in the pure value of creativity as well. In the face of humanists' frequent attempts to "justify the significance of their work by appeal to scientific notions of progress or contributions to society" (Cvetkovich 22), she suggests that "a commitment to creativity, or to pursuing one's own ways of thinking and being, can be salutary" (Cvetkovich 22). Reparative writing thus has value even when that value lies in precisely its nonargumentative explorations of creativity, of the nonevent, of the mundane, the ordinary.

The idea that creative and personal expression can be "productive" in the realm of academic discourse diverges sharply from the demands of paranoid criticism—the demand that scholarship should be limited to the endeavor of proving or revealing aspects of texts and contexts to the exclusion of the scholar's own feeling's about the topic at hand. Indeed, the strongest case studies that Cvetkovich presents to illustrate her argument that depression is a social and cultural feeling is her readings of other examples of life writing in her chapter on racism and depression. She quotes the incredibly poignant line from Anna Deveare Smith's *Twilight: Los Angeles*, which in turn quotes Cornel West saying "But if whites experienced black sadness… (*Pause*)/ It would be too overwhelming for them. (*Pause*)… it's a very very very different kind of/ Sadness" (Cvetkovich 115). Cvetkovich goes on to read four memoirs, two by black writers and two by white writers, the most relevant of which for this project is Saidiya Hartman's *Lose Your Mother*.[7] While Hartman's focus is on the archives of slavery and the ways in which its history infiltrates her own sense of being in the world, she models the kind of reparative writing that Cvetkovich, in writing about her, does as well. Cvetkovich says of her chapter on race that "my goal is to mix it up… in order to cross the color line and make a case for a racialized understanding of depression that draws on different kinds of writing, including fusions of memoir and scholarship" (121), and she observes that for Hartman, "memoir [is] a research method" (126). The combination of the comprehensive research Hartman presents on the slave trade, slavery, and its afterlife on the one hand, and her own feelings of despair and melancholy, on the other, makes for a powerful illustration of how a scholar's memories and emotions are in fact integral to intellectual work.

Inspired by Hartman and others, Cvetkovich begins her study with the established practice of criticizing and revealing underlying assumptions of several popular books about depression, "all of which largely, if ambivalently, endorse pharmaceutical treatment" (Cvetkovich 23).[8] However, she does not stop there; she makes the move from paranoid to reparative writing in her use of academic memoir. As she puts it, "I decided that rather than critique memoir it would be more useful to engage in it as a form of research method" (Cvetkovich 23–24), and this is what she does by including her "depression journals" in a book which is largely written in a quite intimate first-person voice. The "depression journals" form some forty pages of the book and, like Halley's memoirs, they appear in a distinct and blocky sans serif font. The journals chronicle Cvetkovich's descents into and struggles with depression as well as her coping mechanisms. Perhaps the most effective feature of the journals is that they detail the quotidian, the everyday experience that so rarely finds expression in criticism. For example, she details her inability, during one period, to enact small, daily tasks: getting up, buying groceries, going to the dentist, writing a thank you note. While indecisiveness and spending long periods of time in bed may be well-known symptoms of depression, "the lived experience has many nuances not captured by colloquial expressions and abstract diagnoses" (Cvetkovich 44). She describes how the buzz of the alarm clock comes to lack "urgency and meaning" (Cvetkovich 44), and how a trip to the grocery store becomes "excruciating, providing a mocking reminder that I was incapable of even the simplest task" (Cvetkovich 45). Thus, she brings her readers into experiences that do not draw upon or reify academic, medical, or popular works on depression but emerge from the affective archive of Cvetkovich's own memories of depression.

The "Depression Journals" explore the profoundly physical experience of depression, in addition to its more obvious emotional textures. In describing an experience of writer's block that follows a descent into depression, Cvetkovich recalls leaving her desk to "lie on the living room floor, hoping the brief respite would allow my beating heart to still itself. Everything seemed so quiet and ordinary; why was I so terrified?" (Cvetkovich 32). Similarly, she records the embodied manifestations of the anxiety that sets in as she starts a new job: in addition to chronic fatigue, she experiences "a mid-back ache that would not go away, persistent headaches, a furiously beating heart. Downtime, especially at the end of teaching days when I could give myself a break, was filled with fear, or tears, or a dull blankness" (Cvetkovich 34). Lest these details appear solipsistic, she is careful to embed her memories in a larger narrative of "political depression" that she and her collaborators in "public feelings" projects found that they shared in the face of "the sense that customary political response, including direct action and critical analysis, are no longer working to either change the world or make us feel better" (Cvetkovich 1). By framing the Depression Journals with the concept of political depression, on the one hand, and the search for leverage on it through the method of reparative writing, on the other, Cvetkovich's memories function as vital evidence of personal and political observations. In her brief follow-up chapter to the Depression Journals, "Reflections: Memoir as Public Feelings Research Method," she like Halley argues that memoir is a key method of seeing that which is normalized: "the story is about daily life and about how anxiety and what gets called depression are ordinary feelings embedded in ordinary circumstances" (Cvetkovich 79). This is to say that memory is a site of the social that serves as an important source for critical work.

Whereas Cvetkovich and Halley arrange their texts into discrete blocks of memoir within the scope of larger academic projects, a kindred spirit, Elspeth Probyn, employs her memories as a less distinct but equally important dimension of her methodology. In *Blush: Faces of Shame*, she explores the shame affect through a first-person voice that draws on her own experiences of shame in order to advance her study of its social and psychological roles. She says as much in her presentation of her project, which she describes thus: "there are stories and more stories—some of them mine, others that I retell from academic and literary sources... My stories are told in the spirit of experimentation: wouldn't it be interesting if we could all talk about shame in more productive ways?" (xiv–xv). Like Halley, she uses the term "experimental" to classify her genre of writing, and like Halley's exploration of an emotional experience that is resistant to language in the first place—trauma—Probyn's subject of shame makes particular demands on language. Consider the idioms surrounding the shame experience: one wants to disappear, to sink through the floor, to die on the spot, to be invisible, and so forth. These expressions of self-erasure indicate the silences that surround shameful events and acts—events and acts that one wishes to forget but that relentlessly reassert themselves in memory, as we will see in the chapter of this book that deals with the shameful history of slavery in the Americas and the failures and challenges of representing that history.

Probyn opens with the personal memory of opening an email from an esteemed colleague who took her to task for a piece she had published—and rightly so, by her own estimation. Upon reading the message, Probyn blushes, even in the privacy of her own study halfway across the globe from her colleague. Her body registers the betrayal of which she is accused in such a way that she has no recourse to rationalization, to *thinking* away her responsibility to others. Shame is too primal and autonomous an affect to be separated from cognition, and as such it registers within consciousness through the body. She further illustrates the physiological nature of shame by reaching farther into her memory to a moment in her childhood when she made another girl cry. She shows how she felt the burn of shame equally for being caught in the wrong and for making someone else feel wrong about herself. She does not remember how or why she inflicted shame on the other girl, but rather how ashamed she felt for doing harm to another. She can still feel the inner cringe that this memory triggers, and her attention to the physiology of shame drives her experimentation with what she refers to as her "embodied research method."

Probyn is thus clear about how her own affects form a basis of her research, an approach in keeping with my argument that researchers are increasingly drawing on an affective archive in their studies of affect itself. In the spirit of Cvetkovich's Public Feelings, Halley's sociological approach to memory, and Foucault's theory of how power flows through individuals and society, she offers her memories not as confessions but as evidence. She notes the stigma on recording one's lived experiences in academic writing and counters that she "want[s] to move away from the idea that telling shameful stories is concerned only with the person telling them" (Probyn 40). Moreover, she provides an example of the geopolitics of feelings in recounting a memory that immersed her in the national racial history of Australia, where she lives and works. She identifies a particular feeling that structures her own consciousness and that informs her affective responses to place more generally, a feeling she names "out-of-placeness." This feeling arises from her nomadic childhood and early adulthood in multiple regions of Canada, Germany, Wales, and finally Australia, and it persists through her understanding of her tenuous right to walk Australian soil given that country's racial history. She presents one memory in particular as the hinge between her personal and geopolitical positions: the memory of visiting Australia's iconic Uluru, or Ayers Rock. She weeps upon first sighting the rock, and reflects that "that feeling reverberated; it still does. It can't be lifted from other experiences along the road and wasn't quite a distillation of feelings either. It was a white-hot intensity that burned through layers of memory and perception. I have never felt so out of place in my life or so simultaneously desired to be a part of that place" (Probyn 44). The conjunction of her own sense of placelessness with the massive, physical symbol of the Australian land mass reveals the limits of her own white body's "habitus"; she explains how "Our bodies seem to know when they are at ease in a situation, when they know the rules and expectations, and conversely they also tell me when we are out of our league, fish out of water" (Probyn 49). Her comment works as the flip side of Halley's observation that her family members could not perceive the violence that eclipsed their lives because they were as close to it as "fish to water."

Probyn's argument is ultimately that the shame affect is one of the few feelings that can point, from the site of an internal and autonomous moral compass, to otherwise invisible forms of injustice—an argument that, however partial and conditional, is aptly illustrated in her breakdown in the shadow of Uluru.[9] The white-hot feeling that lashes her body is the feeling of her own "shame, which referred itself back to more shame" (Probyn 72)—a national shame that as a white immigrant to Australia she never guessed resided within her. She traces this overwhelming feeling back to the racialized history of bodies and land whereby white bodies are "scratches" on the land in contrast to the kinship between Aboriginal bodies and place. Her point is to look beyond proverbial "white guilt" to recognize something much more intimate, something that cannot be exorcized as can guilt, and that is historical, inherited, ancestral shame that invades even the non-native white body in a place where whites enacted violence against Aboriginal people. She draws on Kim Mahood's account of her own white body reacting to the land as a tropism; the body takes over. Like Probyn's white-hot feeling, Mahood describes "feel[ing] something in my bones and nerves and viscera. I would not describe it as an emotion. It is more like a chemical reaction, as if a certain light and temperature and chemical dryness triggers a series of physical and nervous realignments" (in Probyn 67).[10] This history of the land on which she stands enters Probyn's consciousness not as such, but rather as a distant *memory,* a more personal form of knowledge, and one that enacts a sense of responsibility. This inherited memory lies inside of Probyn, locked away in an inaccessible archive of feelings, until the key of shame unlocks the connection between her enmeshment in another national history and its shameful secrets. That is, through what I would term a Glissantian notion of "the poetics of relation," she links her feeling of shame in Australia to an inherited, ancestral memory of her Canadian grandmother's identification with indigenous people, an identification that veered toward cultural appropriation in, for example, her grandmother's poem entitled "Half Breed." By connecting these different personal narratives of racial and ethnic feelings, lodged as the feelings are in colonial histories, Probyn shows how her feelings of shame flow from multiple national, familial, racial, and geopolitical sites, and how those feelings both give rise to and form a deeply personal understanding of the past. In order to explain the subject of her study, shame, she has to revisit, interrogate, trace, and explore her own memories, which then become invaluable resources in her academic project.

As she argues in her concluding reflections on her embodied research methods, "the body of the writer becomes the battle-ground where ideas and experiences collide, sometimes to produce new visions of life" (Probyn 152). She substantiates this point by recording the suffering that her own body sustained during the writing of *Blush: Faces of Shame*. Proving first-hand that shame is an all-consuming affect, she shares just how painful it was to write about such a devastating feeling, from her sense of anxiety about the project to her experiences of waking up with aching hands and feet after clenching her body in her sleep, in a coil of stress and fear. Her fear stems from the anxiety that her account of shame will not be equal to her interest in its power and function. What if her book fails to capture its subject? What if her writing is inadequate to the task of representing it? The stress that invades her body at night stems from her forays into her own shameful memories, for as anyone who has ever felt ashamed—which is to say everyone—knows, the memory of shame invades the body whether through a blush or raised temperature, muscular tension, or a sudden shakiness.

This example of her "embodied research method" resonates with Cvetkovich's description of her physical breakdown as she dealt with depression, and Halley's account of starving herself as an adolescent in response to her experience of trauma. All embodied research methods, these remembered stories of the body as source and subject of academic research point to a major affective dimension thereof. Probyn's account of coming to the study of shame with her body as well as her mind works as a critique of academic writing that strives to assert objective detachment, especially when what is being studied is emotion itself.

She points out that "the gulf between research and writing is becoming especially fraught with the increase in academic studies about emotions and affects" (Probyn 133). The classic, "paranoid" mode of critical writing could debunk sources of shame and expose the harm they inflict, but such an account would stop short of conveying to the reader the psychological damage, physical suffering, and irrepressible intelligence linked to shame. Probyn's reparative mode of opening herself up to her own memories and feelings of shame fill out her scholarly argument that shame has a social function.

In closing this chapter, I want to acknowledge a curious dimension of writing it, which is that I extoll the methods of writers whose example I do not follow. In this age of social media, I shudder to share, and I have little interest in broadcasting my feelings or opinions to the general public or even the curated public of my Facebook friends. I admit that I am more comfortable writing traditional academic prose and I doubt I will ever write out my own memories for public consumption. Sedgwick, too, in "Paranoid Reading and Reparative Reading," writes in a more or less conventionally impersonal academic voice even as she shows us how to open up texts as reparative readers. As Heather Love notes in her reading of the essay, Sedgwick makes room for both paranoid and reparative reading even as she identifies a tension between the two positions in the interest of illuminating the latter. Thus Sedgwick really does lay out the method of reparative reading, not that of reparative writing, so we can appreciate experimental, reparative writing as an extension of her ideas. Sedgwick notes that "the desire of a reparative impulse… is additive and accretive. Its fear, a realistic one, is that the culture surrounding it is inadequate or inimical to its nurture; it wants to assemble and confer plenitude on an object that will then have resources to offer to an inchoate self" (Sedgwick 149). The plenitude of resources for understanding their subjects of study therefore include the affective archive of the body, of feelings, and of memory, and reparative writing makes room for all of these elements in a way that more conventional or limited discourses do not.

Finally, both Cvetkovich and Halley also position affective memory as not only a site of the social, but as a site of resistance. In her final lines, Halley hopes that her book will be a "crack in the wall of power" (Halley 160), and Cvetkovich opens with the goal of "investigating the productive possibilities of depression" (Cvetkovich 14), suggesting that by exploring "the feeling of remaining or resting in sadness without insisting that it be transformed or reconceived" (Cvetkovich 14), we might gain leverage on the underlying political and social forces that are coextensive with such feelings. Similarly, Probyn's Foucaultian analysis of her own memories and feelings in the context of historical dynamics of power shows them to be volatile disruptions in the fabric of national schemas of remembering and forgetting. Put another way, they offer the hope that their writing will effect change in readers and their communities, and as Sedgwick notes, "Hope, often a fracturing, even a traumatic thing to experience, is among the energies by which the reparatively positioned reader tries to organize the fragments and part-objects she encounters or creates"; hope also gives "the reader... room to realize that the future may be different from the present" (Sedgwick 146) rather than trapping her into historicizing the present through the past. That our writers use affective fragments from the past—memories—in order to crack open new possibilities speaks to their assemblage of different temporal fragments into the form of affective possibility. This display of memories as illuminations of collective feelings, past and present, is an approach that all three writers bring to bear on major social manifestations of depression, gendered violence, and shame as public or social feelings that can only be understood through experimental writing that intertwines affective and archival research. The writers' openness to these erstwhile "negative" feelings presents us with a reparative mode of writing from which to chart a new direction in studying affect.

NOTES

1. The field of anthropology moved in the direction of incorporating subjective experience into academic writing as it came to terms with the culturally and racially biased foundations of ethnography as a genre that developed in lockstep with colonial exploration. As early as the late 1980s and early 1990s, anthropologists such as James Clifford and Renato Rosaldo theorized and wrote ethnography in such a way that the text encompassed intersubjective experience rather than a subject-object relationship. Thus, the genre of academic memoir arguably has roots in experimental forms of ethnography—which have now branched into a body of work that includes "autoethnography," a genre that is very closely related to the kind of affect studies I explore in this chapter.

2. Suzette Henke has proposed a similarly useful concept of reparative writing in the context of autofiction. Coining the term "scriptotherapy,"

Henke demonstrates how women writers work to repair the damage of trauma through fictionalized accounts of their experiences that empower them as witnesses.

3. Johnson, Erica L. *Caribbean Ghostwriting*. Teaneck, NJ and London: Fairleigh Dickinson University Press and Associated University Presses, 2009.

4. Stoler's work may be the best response to Sara Edenheim's noteworthy critique of Cvetkovich and others' notion of the queer archive as an "archive of feeling." Edenheim suggests that Cvetkovich's distinction between a "scholarly" and "queer" archive is false: "the scholar's archive may well be seen as a phantasmatic projection that radicalizes the queer archive of feelings" (Edenheim 41).

5. Much of this section on Halley is taken from my review of her book for *Qualitative Inquiry* (1–3, 2016).

6. Here, Halley cites a study by Amy J. Fitzgerald, Linda Kalof, and Thomas Dietz, "Slaughterhouses and increased crime rates: An Empirical Analysis of the Spillover from 'The Jungle' Into the Surrounding Community." *Organization & Environment* 22.2 (2009): 158–184.

7. Although Hartman's *Lose Your Mother* does not set out to study affect in the ways that my other primary sources do, it is an absolutely essential illustration of cultural memory and how affective and archival work complement one another.

8. Cvetkovich notes William Styron's *Darkness Visible*, Andrew Solomon's *The Noonday Demon*, Elizabeth Wurtzel's *Prozac Nation*, and Lauran Slater's *Prozac Diary* as examples of mainstream works about depression that she finds dissatisfying.

9. Herein lies the controversial nature of Probyn's presentation of shame. Her emphasis on the positive, productive valence of shame as a moral compass is convincing, but she does not deal fully with the role that shame plays in orchestrating every form of social oppression: from "body shaming" to racism, homophobia, sexism, ableism, ageism, and so forth, people have suffered the pain of externally inflicted and internalized shame about how they are embodied. This version of shame is purely negative and oppressive unless and until it is routed back to the shamer, rather than the shamed, as the source of that awful feeling.

10. Rosemary Dalziell also explores the national inheritance of shame in Australian writing in *Shameful Autobiographies: Shame in Contemporary Australian Autobiographies and Culture* (Melbourne: Melbourne University Press, 1999).

CHAPTER 3

Memoir and Memory-Traces

Abstract This chapter focuses on two Caribbean writers who, in keeping with a number of their colleagues, present archival and historical material through their own lived experiences and vice versa. Dionne Brand's memoir recounts her many travels and the ways in which, wherever she is in the world, she sees The Door of No Return as her primary point of reference; in so doing, she draws on an extensive body of literary, cultural, and archival materials alongside her memories of life in Trinidad, Canada, and the many countries to which she has traveled. Patrick Chamoiseau's history of the penal colony of French Guiana is one that he tells through his deeply affective memories of wandering through its ruins. Both case studies demonstrate keen uses of personal memory and experience as essential sources of knowledge.

Keywords Memoir · Ruins · Diaspora · Caribbean

The critics I explored in Chapter 1 draw on memoir in different ways, ranging from academic memoir to other uses of personal memories as material for academic inquiry. Memoir, then, forms a key generic role in works that engage the affective archive, and this chapter will look at the work of memoir more directly. Moreover, the memoir work—and I emphasize the idea of "memoir work" over "memoir" because both of the texts I read here are generically complex—on which I focus are

© The Author(s) 2018
E. L. Johnson, *Cultural Memory, Memorials, and Reparative
Writing*, Palgrave Studies in Affect Theory and Literary Criticism,
https://doi.org/10.1007/978-3-030-02098-9_3

33

rooted in the Caribbean, a region that has produced a body of literature that is profoundly engaged with history and with memory. The explosion of Caribbean writing in the twentieth and twenty-first centuries was sparked in no small part by a need to creatively and imaginatively recoup histories that had been silenced by the colonial archive. For example, C. L. R. James's historical work of the 1930s, including *The Black Jacobins*, covers the history of the Haitian Revolution within the philosophical framework of revolutionary France and within the economic context of the plantation system of the Caribbean, and Selwyn Cudjoe's foundational work of Caribbean literary criticism, *Resistance and Caribbean Literature* (1982), presents literary and historical representation as an intertwined Caribbean poetics. Edouard Glissant followed up on such work in his *Caribbean Discourse* (1986), in which he shows how the violent history of the region disrupts temporal and spatial patterns of representation so that Caribbean literature stages a distinct discourse of historically engaged, disrupted, and disruptive poetics. Maeve McCusker sums up the role of memory in Caribbean writing nicely when she notes its paradoxical but central dynamic: "despite the frequent proclamation by Antillean writers that memory has been erased, repressed or shattered, it remains their most persistent preoccupation, central, as both source and theme, to their literary output" (McCusker 3). McCusker attributes this investment in memory as a response to "the unusually complete decimation of any historical trace of the past" (McCusker 8), a point that certainly fuels the texts that I will explore here. Caribbean memoir work delves into a historically situated form of memory as we see in Dionne Brand's account of her childhood in Trinidad and her adulthood in Canada in *A Map to the Door of No Return: Notes on Belonging*. Similarly, Martinican author Patrick Chamoiseau draws on memory as a form of history in his *Guyane: Traces-mémoires du bagne* [French Guiana: Memory-traces of the Penal Colony], a work that does memoir work by using as source material the author's affective memories of the history of French Guiana's penal colony.[1]

These two texts have much in common, from their shared historical engagements to their mutually dense, lush aesthetic. Both are written in short fragments that hop nimbly from observation to memory to reflection. And, whereas Brand's memoir is classifiable as such and Chamoiseau's text was published as a historical document by the imprint of the national French agency, "Caisse nationale des monuments historiques et des sites," the two authors embed their emotional and physical connections to history in their works. Chamoiseau is present in his text, in that his memory and feelings mediate the story that he tells about the penal colony, whereas even in her memoir Brand writes primarily in the voice of a scholar, a poet, and an observer of histories. To that point, she concludes that she has offered "a life of conversations about a forgotten list of irretrievable selves" (Brand 224), a provocative ending for a memoir, a genre designed specifically to retrieve and represent subjectivity. Brand and Chamoiseau position themselves between their fragments of text and the gaps on the page between them, with Brand offering memories alongside her readings of archival and literary texts, and Chamoiseau disclosing little of his own life but much about his feelings and the workings of memory as he understands and experiences it.

What is more, Brand and Chamoiseau's aesthetic calls for reparative reading. In the Chapter 1, I explored methods of reparative writing by affect theorists, and in this one we'll turn to this method of reading which departs from what Sedgwick identifies as "paranoid" reading, or an approach that seeks to debunk ideological structures in a text. Reparative reading is particularly appropriate to work in affect theory, in light of Sedgwick's foundational work in that field and in light of the fact that attention to affect leads readers and writers alike to attend to aspects of texts that supersede cognitive and intellectual communication. In many ways, the most effective means of conveying Brand's and Chamoiseau's affective accomplishments would be to mirror them, or to witness them—as opposed to parsing and analyzing them. Brand says as much in her observation that "This self which is unobservable is a mystery. It is imprisoned in the observed. It is constantly struggling to wrest itself from the warp of its public ownerships. Its own language is plain yet secret. Rather, obscured" (Brand 51). Given that she claims the illegibility of the self as the subject of a memoir, Brand challenges her reader to accommodate the text's secrets as such—a method of reading that flies in the face of literary exegesis and that requires a stance of affective acceptance.

Reparative reading also performs the task of listening, and in so doing could be classified as "non-representational," as Nigel Thrift explains in *Non-Representational Theory*. This phenomenological approach seeks to capture "the lived immediacy of actual experience, before any reflection on it" (Thrift 6). The goal is to appreciate that "human life is based in and on movement" (Thrift 5), and to "think of the leitmotif of movement as a desire for presence which escapes a consciousness-centered core of self-reference" (Thrift 5). While Thrift's subject matter is human geography, his theory applies to the study of texts as aesthetically immediate and as thematically concerned with history-as-lived-experience as *Guyane: Traces-mémoires du bagne* and *A Map to the Door of No Return.* Thrift's non-representational theory suggests a mode of listening as analysis. In other words, it is as important for the critic to re-present texts as it is to explicate them, and I therefore seek to manifest Brand's and Chamoiseau's writing as well as to present an argument about the extent to which they present memory as a mobile and embodied concept. In an explanation of the uses of non-representational theory, L. Cadman suggests that "Non-representational thinking tends toward an academic style which seeks to describe and present rather than diagnose and represent" (Cadman 461). Cadman could be describing Brand's and Chamoiseau's own writing strategy as well as my approach to their writing. Whereas most forms of criticism seek to reveal the mystery of undocumented histories, non-representational theory approaches the material of the unconscious, discursive structures, and invisible genealogies as points of reference rather than as subjects of analysis.

Melissa Gregg lays out a similar approach in *Cultural Studies' Affective Voices,* in which she explores her own process of "sympathetic reading" and espouses a stance of "intellectual hospitality" toward texts. With this disposition in mind, she seeks to illuminate "the affective properties of scholarly voices [which] offer the chance to spread conceptual advances and theoretical insights further than might otherwise be the case" (Gregg 19). Gregg focuses on theoretical texts in the field of cultural studies, but her point is even more à propos of texts that mesh creative and theoretical expression such as Chamoiseau's and Brand's, for *Guyane* and *A Map to the Door of No Return,* seek to draw the reader into the poetic force of the writers' encounters with history. One is meant to feel the shock of the authors' encounters with violence and ruins, and to "feel backward" toward the different registers of history that they evoke in their prose. Gregg offers the helpful concept of "mimetic doubles" in order to articulate the relationship between reader and writer around such complex texts. "The mimetic double begins as a response to a stimulus (a tracing of the text) but comes into its own as a work of criticism through the idiosyncrasy of the gestures it notices" (Gregg 13).

It is a bit intimidating to pose oneself as the mimetic double of either author's intensely rich, complicated, and emotional language. This is all the more so because they write in the face of silence, of "mémoires asphyxiés" [suffocated memories] and "histoires souterraines" [underground histories] (Chamoiseau 15), and the corresponding *absence* of archives or memorials. Brand establishes silence as a point of origin for her memoir in her use of the Door of No Return, the figurative and literal ruin of the slave-trading fortresses on the west coast of Africa, as her guiding star. She writes, "the door exists as an absence. A thing in fact which we do not know about, a place we do not know. Yet... every gesture our bodies make somehow gestures toward this door" (Brand 25). Both writers, then, work within a representational framework of absence, a framework that evokes and listens to the past as much as it recounts histories. The mysteries remain and their pull on that which can be observed is as powerful as ever, which means they are transformed into affective material, leaving the surface-depth binary that structures so much of analytical thought to be reconfigured as an unbounded flow that is expressed in writing.

DIONNE BRAND'S COUNTERMEMORIES

I have written elsewhere about *A Map to the Door of No Return* as a key contributor to what I called the "neo-archive."[2] In that article, I look at how Brand's memoir incorporates supporting materials that range from the sixteenth-century logs and newspaper articles to literature and pop culture. As I note in the introduction, her sources can be broken down into the three general categories of historical archives written during the "age of exploration" and the slave trade; the contemporary archives of newspapers and journals; and the creative archive of post-colonial writers, or what I call the neo-archive. While letters and journals of explorers, ships' logs, and print journalism alike are available through archival research, the histories presented in such novels as Toni Morrison's *Beloved* and in the poetry of Aimé Césaire, Eduardo Galeano, and Derek Walcott are accessible through creativity and imagination. I now want to focus on the extent to which Brand not only uses a neo-archive as source material for her memoir but also contributes to the neo-archive with her own affective memories, given how closely linked memory and history are in her work. Together with Chamoiseau and other writers who enter the gaps of the archives, Brand represents traumatic and silenced histories through the feelings they provoke in her as a memoirist.

In effect, Brand presents memory as just as fallible and incomplete as the colonial histories to which she traces her genealogy, a scenario that necessitates her historical interventions. She does the same historical work in the form of a memoir that Tavia Nyong'o says he seeks to do in his memoir-inflected academic writing:

> My method employs the archives as a practice of 'countermemory' but without the pretense of using it to build a complete or coherent historical narrative. The form of hybrid and performative historiography I have adopted is intended to subvert the expected hermeneutic cycle of traditional archival research, interpretation, and explication. I seek to both assert and show the performative affects of history rather than simply to add to the weight of history's pedagogy. (Nyong'o 7)

This combination of archival research and affective performance underscores Brand's writing as well. For example, she turns to Charles Bricker's *Landmarks of Mapmaking* in her research into her ancestors' African past, and in it she finds "explorers, sailing along the coast, called what they did not or could not see deep and dark, moving inland little by little toward their own fears" (Brand 17). The maps in the book are not just materials for cognitive orientation; they map as well feelings of fear and forgetting. As a result of these map and history-making processes, the "African self... was informed by colonial images of the African as savage and not by anything we could call on our memories to conjure" (Brand 17). The feelings of the mapmakers and of the reader of those maps disclose vital information about the historical encounters that haunt Brand's memoir. Moreover, they make her into a mapmaker herself: "I am constructing a map of the region, paying attention to faces, to the unknowable, to unintended acts of returning, to impressions of doorways" (Brand 19). Brand's map charts the African continent palimpsestically: over the backdrop of the explorers' maps of anxiety and avarice, she charts her own feelings of loss and forgetting with the result that she uses maps as what Nyong'o calls countermemories. That is, the maps of the archives are not building blocks of history but rather performances of a world view that Brand incorporates into her own mapping of Diaspora.

Brand's strategy of threading her memories through archival materials resonates with Nyong'o's method as well. He could have been describing *A Map* when he says, "Taking up the popular pedagogical tropes of historical and embodied memory, I invert the traditional distinction between textual archives and embodied memories by examining collective memory as a 'texted' or encoded structure, one prone to the same glitches and errors of transmission as the fallible, falsifiable archive" (Nyong'o 9). This enmeshment of body and text is one that Brand expresses repeatedly, in such elegant aphorisms as this one: "To have one's belonging lodged in a metaphor is voluptuous intrigue; to inhabit a trope; to be a kind of fiction..." (Brand 19). If she feels herself to be a textual being, that is because she inhabits and performs texts—which means that there is a feedback loop between textuality and embodied experience. Omise'eke Natasha Tinsley remarks on this dynamic of the text in her queer reading of it, in which she notes that "Brand plumb[s] the archival ocean materially, as space that churns with physical remnants, dis(re)membered bodies of the Middle Passage, and [she] plumb[s] it metaphorically, as opaque space to convey the drowned, dis-remembered, ebbing and flowing histories of violence and healing in the African diaspora" (Tinsley 194). By including the ocean as an archival source, Tinsley, like Nyong'o, expands on the category of the archive to include natural and embodied sites of history. Brand's affective engagement with the archive and its proliferating postcolonial forms is one that Michael Laramie observes as well, in his note that in Brand's writing "the use of one's senses and emotions in navigating through the Door of No Return and into the empty room where history awaits and fashions itself is crucial" (Laramie np). Sensory and emotional registers of knowledge connect with other epistemes through the extensive research that Brand offers in her pages, but they connect through the embodiment of the researcher as well.

And indeed the body is front and center in Brand's writing. She says, for example, "I remember [the books] only in my body" (Brand 192) and she returns several times to the theme of bodies in motion that she captures in her statement that "My body feels always in the middle of a journey" (Brand 54). There is a literal truth to this statement for the author, who travels between England, Trinidad, Dominica, St. Lucia, Grenada, Vancouver, Australia, Amsterdam, Toronto, South Africa, and other destinations in the course of her memoir. She thereby situates the subject of the text in the air, above the land upon which she lights from time to time.[3] More importantly, though, the journey's function as not only a progression toward arrival but as a site of departure is a key concept of the memoir's early chapters which dwell on what it means to have to trace one's past back to the Door of No Return. As the threshold on the West African coast through which millions of enslaved people passed on their way to the Americas, the Door of No Return is terribly real in a historical sense yet, Brand says, it "exists as an absence" (Brand 25). As a result, the door palpably haunts her as an unwelcome specter of historical violence and ruptured memory. It bars her family's knowledge of their ancestry, as she demonstrates in several fragments in which she probes her grandfather, in vain, for answers to her questions about their relationship to various African civilizations. Jody Mason observes the paradoxical status of the Door thus: "it is both the place where enslaved Africans bestowed the gift of forgetting on their descendants and the place where those descendants can create from the minus in the origin" (Mason np). Yet what Brand emphasizes about the Door is not just its status as a wound, for she also explores its role as a "passport": "We arrive with its coat of arms, its love knot, its streamers, its bugle, its emblem attesting to our impossible origins. This passport is from the territory of the Door. The territory is vast, its nature shiftable. *We are always in the middle of the journey*" (Brand 48–9, emphasis added). In this passage, Brand captures the paradox of the door in its foreclosure of origins and its launching of journeys. Moreover, her use of the passport metaphor introduces a new set of complexities to the journeys, for passports both provide and block access to the world depending on which passport one carries into which territories. Passports also allude to origins without being affixed to them, for citizenship can change and multiply as Brand demonstrates in her own migration from Trinidad to Canada, and in her novels which always include migration as a theme.

With the wound of the Door as a passport, Brand presents materials that speak to black experience in the Diaspora, among which she situates her own memories. Ayn Becze explains Brand's "process" as one in which "memory functions synchronically and diachronically to recall the heterogeneous identity of Blacks in history, politics, and literature" (Becze np). Brand thus summons up cultural memories as well as personal ones, and she does this through her use of various media sources. In one example of this strategy, she splices together pieces of newspaper articles published in 2000: one from the *Guardian Weekly* about African migrants being assaulted and killed by police officers in Austria, one from the *New York Times* about the vicious police attacks on Abner Louima, and one from *Time* magazine about the police shooting of Amadou Diallo. She does not comment directly on any of the excerpts; instead,

Brand links them through adjacency, and in so doing she connects the articles with historical instances of violence done to black bodies and "other bodies in the world which are brutalized," ranging from women in Afghanistan to the "spectres... revived... in Bosnia" (Brand 48). In effect, she mobilizes memory. Rather than reconstructing the past, she presses it onto the present. As Maureen Moynagh observes of texts that cope with the legacy of slavery and its attendant racism, these works "comprise a literary corpus that dominant narratives of modernity have refused to accommodate" (Moynagh 57), and she observes the melancholic structures in Brand's writing that work to keep the door to the past ajar. Indeed, Brand shows the limits of historical and contemporary narratives alike, and her presentation of the newspaper clippings reopen rather than close the cases that they recount. The news fragments tell three different stories, but those stories animate one another, as well as the other pieces of evidence Brand offers that point her back to the Door of No Return as a driving narrative force that unleashes scattered stories in the first place.

And, as the archival fragments animate one another, Brand's own memories spark and are sparked by her engagement with such texts. Memory thus mingles with history to form a third source of knowledge about the past. Most of Brand's memories are of encounters she has as a traveller: an encounter with a parking attendant as she heads into a reading, an encounter with a seethingly hostile local man near her cabin in rural Canada, an encounter with children in Trinidad who make her feel their perfect homeliness and her own dislocation. But there is one personal memory which, because it is a memory of trauma, haunts the book, and that is Brand's memory of the violent end of the New Jewel Movement in Grenada in the 1980s. She had travelled there to find a safe space among other black political activists, and her first novel, *In Another Place, Not Here*, grew out of her experiences and even includes the scene of trauma which she describes in *A Map*. She witnessed, from her balcony, the attack of the U.S. army on a gathering of activists that she had left just minutes before the assault, little suspecting what would happen. From a distance, she saw tanks mow down people she loved, many of whom fell down a steep cliff by the fort: "The crowd where I had been standing began running in all directions. I saw people leap from the cliff and bump raggedly down its side. There was nowhere to run... The air dropped from my own body, there were a thousand bright stab wounds in my skin" (Brand 165). The embodiment of this memory continues in her description of how, during later bombing raids, "Your body cracks to each sound of gunfire… By the time it's over you are brittle, your teeth feel like crushed stones, you are skeletal, you have a single wire of electricity running up your back over which you have no control. That is only the corporeal" (Brand 168). Brand's corporeal memory of Grenadians under attack stands beside her many, many articles of evidence of brutality against black bodies throughout the memoir. She is able to bring this memory into evidence in much the same way that she summons the story of Amadou Diallo and the stories of racial violence in Morrison's *Paradise* and J. M. Coetzee's *Disgrace*. Weaving memory, archive, and neo-archive together, Brand presents a deeply affecting portrait of, as Cvetkovich says, *"what diaspora feels like"*.

THE CREOLIZATION OF MEMORY

Like Brand, the Martinican author Patrick Chamoiseau writes between genres in *Guyane: Traces-mémoires du bagne*. He is a novelist, a memoirist, and a theorist, and in a number of texts these genres overlap in much the same way that theory and memoir come together in the works I explored in Chapter 1. Like those affect theory scholars who present memory as an important archival source in their experimental writing, Chamoiseau presents affective memory as a crucial medium of doing postcolonial historical work in his hybrid text. Indeed, its hybridity crosses media as well as genres in that the book is composed of photographs by his collaborator, Rodolphe Hammadi, as much as it is by Chamoiseau's prose. Between the melancholic images and the poetic language, *Guyane* offers a deeply affective exploration of the French Guianese penal colony, which endured for a century. In his contribution, Chamoiseau deploys a memory-based methodology that connects to the concept of the "affective archive" that I established in Chapter 1; he also presents a critique of monuments and memorialization that connects to my final chapter on that topic.

Chamoiseau's memory project in *Guyane* is to explore the colonial ruins of the prisons of French Guiana, where criminals and dissidents— including, most famously, Alfred Dreyfuss—were imprisoned as early as 1854 and as late as 1952. Nearly 100,000 inmates passed through the cells and barracks there, yet the historical records of those lives and later accounts are sparse. The bare bones of the history are that after the 1848 revolution, France sought to establish prisons in the colonies, beginning with Algeria, in order to effectively purge political dissidents from France itself. Whereas penal colonies existed in several port cities of France in the nineteenth century, this concept was exported to French Guiana and New Caledonia after 1848. In New Caledonia, the penal policy served the double purpose of creating a settler colony, and after prisoners had served their sentences, their families were able to join them so that they could take up permanent residence there. Early attempts were made to make French Guiana a settler colony as well, but the harsher climate and conditions there undermined that plan.[4] As a result, the penal colony remained a temporary and purely punitive locale for its inmates, the vast majority of whom were repatriated to France or to the other French colonies from whence they came after serving their sentences.

The geography of French Guiana was particularly conducive to sequestration, with its numerous small islands off of the coast—islands that more or less replaced the *bagnes flottantes*, or prison ships that were moored off the coast of France's coastal penal colonies to make escape all the more difficult. The islands, like the *bagnes flottantes*, served as sites of extreme isolation for those deemed unruly or dangerous. What is more, the establishment of penal colonies in the Caribbean coincided with the end of slavery there: French colonies in the Caribbean region had long relied on enslaved labor but with the emancipation decree of 1848, they sought new sources of unpaid labor. The prison system picked up where slavery left off, as did indentured servitude in the British Caribbean and the carceral system in the United States.[5]

That said, *Guyane* stands out in Chamoiseau's oeuvre as one that engages history, as do many of his texts, but not the history of the African diaspora or of the enslaved per se. In contrast to the many novels, memoirs, and films through which Chamoiseau has sought to recoup a representation of slavery and its long shadow, he turns his attention to another form of imprisonment and forced labor in his focus on the penal colony. While prisoners were brought to French Guiana from numerous French colonies including Indochina, Reunion, and Algeria, the majority of the prisoners were ethnically European French nationals. The differential between *Guyane* and his other work is evident in the contrast between it and another collaboration with a photojournalist that he published in 1999, *Traces de mélancolies*, with Jean-Luc de Laguarigue. This later book documents contemporary life in Martinique and its entrenchment in history, and it picks up the notion of the *traces-mémoires* in Chamoiseau's extended meditation on "traces" as signifiers of the unrepresentable and unarchived past. It is precisely the dehumanizing record of the lives of the enslaved that prompts so many Caribbean writers to plunge into history and memory, as we see with Brand's *A Map* and Chamoiseau's film *The Middle Passage* (among many of his works to so engage). In another example, Euridice Figueiredo's analysis of Chamoiseau's novel *Un dimanche au cachot* addresses his use of ruins and archives in this fictional setting: she notes that "considering that the ruins of this *Habitation* [plantation] are a kind of archive that bears the marks, the traces of the treatment given to slaves, Chamoiseau performs an anamnesis as a kind of therapy... as the archive is hipomnesic, that is, a document or monument, the dungeon-ruins function in the novel as an archive" (Figueiredo 254). Figueiredo's rhetoric here is fluent with Chamoiseau's terminology throughout *Guyane*, as both his novel about slavery and his memoir work about the penal colony enact a similar historical project. Therefore, his representation of the *bagne* is in dialogue with such works and it is imbued with important allegorical properties and adjacencies to the telling of slavery; in that he works through many of the ideas that he contextualizes in stories of Africans in the New World elsewhere. His *Guyane* is as much a theorization of how the past *can* be recalled as it is a history of the penal colony itself.

In terms of historical accounts, perhaps the most thorough presentation of the penal colony is Stephen Toth's *Beyond Papillon*, a book that takes its title from the most famous representation of the colony, the 1973 film starring Steve McQueen and Dustin Hoffman. Toth's research is informative, both in terms of filling readers in about the practices, regulations, and so forth, of the *bagne*, and in revealing the opacity of that history. Toth contends that "the history of the *bagne* itself has remained opaque and obscured, caught between myth and monolith" (Toth 150). His study is based on such archival documents as records of transport, cell and labor assignments, and a *livret* that noted each inmate's former profession, work assignment and, oddly, phrenological features. These *livrets* thus worked to efface the prisoners as people while establishing them as *bagnards*, or prisoners. This is characteristic of colonial history, programmed as it is to create a narrative of French superiority—in this case, to "quantify and normalize [the] penal colony... such documents, while allowing the institution to operate in a coldly effective manner, dehumanized the prisoners" (Toth 44–5). Toth alludes here to the paradox of much colonial documentation, in that it obscures the humanity of the very people it catalogs. Archival materials are thus useful but woefully inadequate to the historian, and certainly to a poet-historian such as Chamoiseau.

Following in the footsteps of Glissant, Chamoiseau offers the concept of the "traces-mémoires," or "memory-traces," to counter linear historical narrative in his writing about the penal colony. He also develops his idea of memory-traces in contrast to Pierre Nora's *lieux de mémoires*, or the idea that memory and history, whose distinct properties he contrasts with one another in his opening notes, can converge in certain sites.[6] Whereas Nora's memory sites are meant to invest an individual's memory with a larger (national) history, Chamoiseau argues against such a unifying conceptualization of cultural memory. He sees history in all of its splinters: "Dessous l'Histoire colonial écrite, il faut trouver la trace des histoires" [Beneath written colonial History, one must find the traces of histories] (Chamoiseau 15), and he goes on to explain that a *traces-mémoires* is "un espace oublié par l'Histoire et par la Mémoire-une, car elle témoigne des histoires dominés, des mémoires écrasés, et tend à les preserver" [a space forgotten by History and by monolithic Memory, because it witnesses dominated histories, crushed memories, and works to preserve them]. This is in keeping with his earlier work as an original and influential theorist of *la créolité*, a worldview through which he and his colleagues sought out forms of expression that encompassed the relational poetics of Caribbean ontology. In his co-authored *Éloge de la créolité* [*In Praise of Creoleness*, 1989], the authors write that "Creoleness is our primitive soup and our continuation, our primeval chaos and our mangrove swamp of virtualities" (Chamoiseau et al. 892); in *Guyane*, Chamoiseau writes that his goal is to immerse himself in "un bouillon primordial, une harmonie chaotique dont l'invariant premier demeure *l'émotion du souvenir* du bagne" (Chamoiseau 42) ["a primeval broth, a chaotic harmony whose only constant remains *the emotion of memory* of the penal colony"]. The resonance between his concept of *créolité* and that of *traces-mémoires* can be heard in the metaphors of simmering soups and chaos; just as creoleness is composed of an indeterminate and unbounded mixture of elements, memory-traces reach into the past through diverse passages, some of which are blazed trails and some of which are invisible and internal to the writer. *Éloge de la créolité* explores the "interactional or transactional aggregate" of race, language, religion, and custom, and to that I would add memory. Cultural memory, autobiographical memory, affective memory, memory preserved in the archive, memory erased by the archive, memory-scapes: these diverse forms of recall accompany the linguistic, religious, and racial histories of which the *Éloge*'s authors speak. Memory is creolized in *Guyane: Traces-mémoires du bagne*, in that it is not conscribed to the body, to the archive, or even to cultural memory but rather it functions through different forms and remains fragmented in its inscription. As Chamoiseau puts it, the prisoners' lives are not chronicled in written accounts but rather they "circule dessous l'écriture" [circulate beneath writing] in "la mémoire orale" [oral memory], a dynamic that splinters the notion of Histoire (with a capital h) into *des histoires* and that of Mémoire (with a capital m) into *des mémoires*.

Chamoiseau's poetic interventions into this history draw from his wanderings through the ruins, and the way they spark his imagination and his emotion. As a research method, this approach closely resembles that of Saidiya Hartman in *Lose Your Mother* in the section where she visits slave forts in Ghana in (dashed) hopes of connecting emotionally to lives that may or may not have been those of her ancestors. For Hartman, the ruins do not trigger feelings of connection but rather make her feel all the more lost and detached from her ancestral history. The experience inspires feelings of sadness upon which Hartman meditates and upon which Cvetkovich draws in her analysis of race and depression, as I note in the previous chapter. For Chamoiseau, physical immersion in the ruins of a massive "camp" does result in a form of understanding about the prisoners. For example, he encounters a building labeled "hospital," which he construes as "un havre dans la douleur" [a haven amidst the pain]; he imagines the self-wounding, the self-induced tubercular coughs, that the prisoners might have presented to "bored and suspicious" doctors in order to find even a miserable reprieve from their labors. The walls are now knotted with enormous tree roots that tear up the stones and cement with sap and with outgrowths, and he likens these ruins to those of a slave cemetery he once visited on a plantation in Louisiana—and then he loops back to the Guianese transportation camp, where dungeon walls expel "shadows of dark energy" that contaminate even the encroaching plant life. These memory-traces, then, follow the writer's mind back and forth between the ruins that he witnesses before him and those in his own memory; they grow from his sense of the branching roots beneath the ruins that he sees before him.

In another example, he writes that, "En plongeant dans les histoires du bagne, j'ai trouvé tous les héroïsmes, toutes les dignités, toutes les ferveurs, mais aussi toutes les inhumanités, les dénis agresseurs, le comble des souffrances et des indignités, l'absolu des courages et des faiblesses" (Chamoiseau 19) [In plunging into the histories of the penal colony, I've found all of the heroisms, all of the dignities, all of the passions, but also all of the inhumanities, the harsh denials, the sufferings and indignities, the height of courages and depths of weaknesses]. In Chamoiseauian fashion, his pluralizing of each of these feelings departs with standard discourse, and works to further establish the pluralities of the histories he seeks through his memory work. Moreover, he emphasizes the affective dimensions of the *bagne*, as he does even in his representation of the physical traces of the prisons, of which he says, "les édifices pénitentiaires de l'horreur, accablés par les âges, patinés par le temps, se sont transformés non pas en monuments, main en Traces-mémoires" (Chamoiseau 20) [the penitentiary buildings of horror, stricken by the years, patinaed by time, are transformed not into monuments, but into memory-traces]. The different strands of material history, archival history—to which Chamoiseau refers only in passing—affective memory, and visual reportage all feed into the portrait he offers of the prisons, of the prisoners, and of the country itself.

Moreover, while Brand is overt about the centrality of her body to her memories, her readings, and her observations—"my body feels always in the middle of a journey"—Chamoiseau positions his body as a "réceptacle d'émotion... [une] antenne sensible" (Chamoiseau 25) [a receptacle of emotion; a sensible antenna] without saying as much. Indeed, his method of exploration is to walk among the ruins, to feel the cold cellular air on his skin, to imagine smelling the same sea air and vegetal odors that the prisoners once did. This embodied research method forms a more or less silent layer of his text, but it is the medium through which he connects with his subject matter. *Guyane* would not exist as such, were he to have written from a library or an office: in fact, his entire point is that the history of the *bagne* is unknowable to archival researchers and armchair academics. Rather, it is a history that he entered corporeally in order to craft a text that might grant a reader similarly affective knowledge. It is for this reason that his writing demands to be read reparatively: when he says, for example, that the buildings themselves form "Traces-mémoires, car ils ont été durant de longues années abandonnés dans un face-à-face solitaire avec des fureurs végétales, avec l'emmêlement de racines, l'étouffement des denses ramures" (Chamoiseau 21) [memory-traces, because they endured long years of abandonment in a solitary face-off with vegetal fury, with the tangle of roots, the suffocation of dense twigs], a reader can but receive these material impressions as he offers them. The passage of the writer's body through broken doors and overgrown walls forms the dynamic of the text.

The corporeal and material dimension of the text is captured as well in Hammadi's photographs, for *Guyane* is a visual as well as textual document. In fact, to the thirty-three pages of Chamoiseau's text, there are sixty-seven pages of photographs.[7] For the most part, the images capture overgrown ruins, with tree roots and vines encroaching upon dilapidated walls and rusty bars. A few of the photos document structures that appear to be renovated or preserved in a more solid state, most likely for the parts of the *bagne* that serve as a tourist site—for what Charles Forsdick and others have called "dark tourism." The photos are aesthetically and thematically unified by a color palette (green, rust red, rot brown) and by apertures: the vast majority of the images feature doors and windows. Max Silverman characterizes the photographer's gaze thus: "Hammadi's camera situates the dilapidated buildings of the former penal settlement in their natural surroundings, the focus always shifting and maintaining a tension between the world of the penal colony and the natural world outside and evoking a layering of different time-sequences... [he] grounds the penal colony in the familiar and the everyday, and the present in the past" (Silverman 2009, 26). This strategy of revealing the interconnected layers of the past and the present is very much what Chamoiseau does in his prose, seeking as he does to excavate human experiences and feelings spanning more than a century of the penal colony.

To look at one example of how past and present converge in a photo, Hammadi offers the image of a building that appears to be relatively well preserved, in which there are two doors, labeled "relegués" [conscribed] and "liberés" [free] (Fig. 3.1). The two fates appear to be embodied in the very architecture of the building: the door that indicates freedom opens to the outside landscape and one can see a dirt path and vegetation on the other side, whereas the door for those still in custody opens onto a wall that leads back into the structure of the building. There appears to be a video camera affixed to the wall above the doors, which indicates that this space is likely open to tourists. The effect of the photo is harrowing, in that viewers see the doors from a point of approach, which means that they can imagine and experience what it would be like to pass through the door to freedom or through the door that will take them into a punitive space. Through which door did Chamoiseau pass in

Fig. 3.1   Copyright Rodolphe Hammadi, 1991

his wanderings? We are left with the rough feelings of hope and despair that the image conjures.

Hammadi's photo thus resonates with the written text in all of its cryptic references to suffering and loss, and it invites the reader to sympathetically imagine being in the space that Chamoiseau describes so evocatively but non-mimetically. Indeed, the photographs are a crucial companion to Chamoiseau's attempts to create an affective archive about French Guiana in the dialogue they sustain between the writer's feelings, emotions, and abstractions and the physical reality of the ruins. Silverman observes that, together, "Chamoiseau and Hammadi dissolve the fixed meanings of word and image in the same way that the ruins have transformed the shape, stature and design of the original buildings. The transformation of the fixed monument into the memory-trace is therefore the poetic transformation of word and image into the echoes, resonances, and reverberations of memory" (Silverman 2010, 229). The physical crumbling of the camp into mere traces of its former self works as a powerful metaphor for the lost history. Most information about the prisoners' lives cannot be unearthed, and this lost knowledge is mimetically reflected in the lost rooftops, walls, doors, and windows: both the site and its history lie in ruins. In no small measure, the combined written and visual texts of *Guyane* run in parallel to Brand's project in that the *bagne* and the Door of No Return are at once material sites and powerful allegories. Both are governing tropes of their respective texts.

In another view, taken of an unreconstructed area of the camp, Hammadi's lens peers through an aperture in a wall toward the arched doors and walls that once formed the spine of a now absent building (Fig. 3.2). The series of doorways appears as if one were looking down an infinitely long hallway, or into a mirror that endlessly reflects a passageway. The robust green carpeting of the ruins alleviates feelings of captivity, as does the open sky above the ghostly hallway. Indeed, the natural world's entrance into the structure of the prison serves as a reminder that the ruins belong less to the "built environment" than they do to an environment that is being unbuilt, deconstructed by nature. As a memory-trace, this image is more forceful than any monument, a point that Chamoiseau makes in his observation that "le monument témoigne toujours d'une force dominante enracinée–et verticale" (Chamoiseau 17) [monuments always bear witness to a powerful, rooted and vertical strength] and that when "les peuples créoles américains... se tournent vers les Monuments qui balisent leurs espaces, ils ne s'y retrouvent pas, ou alors, vénérant

Fig. 3.2 Copyright Rodolphe Hammadi, 1991

ces édifices, ils s'aliènér à la Mémoire et à l'Histoire édictées par la colonisation" (Chamoiseau 15) [the American Creole people… turn toward Monuments that mark their spaces, they don't find themselves there, or rather, in venerating these structures, they become alienated by Memory and by History as dictated by the forces of colonization]. In contrast, the ruins themselves form forceful *countermonuments* in the sense that they are memory-traces: "Les edifices de la mort organisée font aujourd'hui Traces-mémoires parce qu'ils proviennent de la mort. Ils ramènent de la mort une opacité qui fait sense, c'est-à-dire: émotions et hoquets de sensations" (Chamoiseau 21) [the buildings of the death camp today form memory-traces because they arise from death. They bring back to death an opacity that can be felt, that is to say: emotions and shocks of sensations]. Hammadi's documentation of the ruins multiplies the text's representation of them—and thus creolizes—Chamoiseau's affective notion of the Traces-mémoires/Memory-traces. In the case of the vanishing hallway, Hammadi positions the viewer as Chamoiseau might have been positioned, as a witness peering onto the ruins through a dark crevice, as though this place is not meant to be seen but, once seen, it becomes evidence of the crimes the witness can now see and feel.

Hammadi's photographs are all eloquent, moving, and integral to Chamoiseau's ideas. I cannot go into all of them, but in a final example that echoes both the endless hallway and potentially even the Door of No Return, let's look at another series of doorways (Fig. 3.3). The photo captures eroding walls illuminated by bright sunshine. While a number of the doorways that Hammadi photographs feature twisted and rusting bars evocative of the prison cells they once were, these doorways are empty and open so that the eye can see through the entire structure to the pathway and other buildings beyond. There is no telling what purpose this particular building served, unlike those that are labeled "hospital" or "workhaus," but there are faint remnants of an iron grill attached to the outside of the doorway. What is moving about this photo, beyond what the viewer can imagine about its role in the penal colony, is that it features a shaggy yellow dog ambling through the rooms. There are animals in several of the photos, including another shot of a dog in front of a fading shack and of a chicken scratching in front of yet another doorway. The living presence of the dog moving through the ruins brings together the past and the present. The animal signifies contemporaneity and the lived experience of the ruins, almost as a proxy for Chamoiseau, who appears in none of the photos. In fact, in contrast

Fig. 3.3   Copyright Rodolphe Hammadi, 1991

to the many portraits of people in Martinique in *Traces de mélancolies*, there are no humans in the photos in *Guyane*. This posthuman aesthetic mimes the absence of the prisoners' individual stories and the fact that such stories can be imagined and intuited but that they defy reconstruction. The extent to which the dog stands in for the writer is also evident, in that Chamoiseau identifies himself not as a "visitor" to the site, but as a wanderer, and this kinesis is also invoked by the idea of the animal's movements, non-deliberate and random as they are. Andy Stafford, too, notes the author's claim to have gone to the *bagne* "not as a visit, but in *errance*, not walking idly through but straying and rambling" (Stafford 33). I would point out, vis-à-vis the photo, that straying and rambling are movements that dogs are said to make. Stafford thus emphasizes the *errance* of both the textual and visual dimensions of *Guyane*, and he points out that the movements of the author and of the camera defy singularity or linearity in their wandering meditations and visions of the ruins. The straying dog in the photo embodies this aesthetic, in that the creature undoes the built environment in much the same way that the plant life that overtakes rooms and buildings throughout the series does. The past is not past, so to speak, but rather its memory-traces are both psychological, as for Chamoiseau, and material, as for the dog.[8]

CONCLUSION: MEMORY, THE TEMPORALITY OF AFFECT

In *Guyane: Traces-mémoires du bagne*, then, Chamoiseau reaches for emotional knowledge of the past since he is deeply skeptical of the form it has assumed in other (French) historical narratives. The work is personal and philosophical in tone, and ultimately what it explores, vis-à-vis this study, is *the temporality of affect* in its use of memory—for memory is a form of affect in itself. Owain Jones and Joanne Garde-Hansen, in *Geography and Memory*, note a creep toward "presentism" in the field of geography, and the same might be said for affect studies. However, they note that "the richness and potential of the present moment in practice comes from what flows into it from previous moments, materially, through the body and… through memory of one kind or another" (Jones and Garde-Hansen 9). Indeed, affect stitches together different tenses and points in time. While we employ memory cognitively in much of our intellectual work, the memories that make us who we are, are affective memories. There is no daylight between one's memory of an important event in one's life, how one felt about it at the time, and how one feels about it at the moment of recall. The memories that undergird our identities and that envelope us unexpectedly do so affectively. As a temporal affect, then, memory serves Chamoiseau as a means of access to history.

Chamoiseau expresses this idea in his inscriptions of the physical and emotional feelings that his visit to the prisons of French Guiana prompted in him. He argues that, far from being legible in existing histories or in the historical monuments that bear limited witness, the history of the region can only be understood by absorbing its landscape and its ruins. He writes that the prison "a balisé notre espace de *Lieux de mémoires,* ou plus exactement de *Traces-mémoires* dont la portée symbolique, *affective,* fonctionelle, dont les significations ouvertes, évolutives, vivantes, dépassent de bien loin l'équation immobile des traditionnels monuments que l'on réportorie dans la Mémoire occidentale" (Chamoiseau 16, emphasis mine) [has marked out *sites of memory,* or more accurately *memory-traces* with their symbolic and *affective* scope, with their open, evolving, living, shifting meanings which far exceed the fixed equation of traditional monuments recorded in Western Memory]. Here, he draws a distinction between the fixed yet incomplete nature of "colonial written history" and "traditional monuments," on the one hand, and the shifting, affective, and evolving histories that saturate the penal colony on the other. As Wendy Knepper puts it with regard to his life writing, memory for Chamoiseau "functions as a deconstructive gesture in which the memory of sensations is inextricably bound up and released through language" (Knepper 134). Similarly, in *Guyane* Chamoiseau conducts a poetic investigation of the ruins of the penal colony through his senses, through his feelings, and through the palpable imagination through which he renders present the pain, desperation, and death that once filled its cells.

Notes

1. Chamoiseau's book has not yet been published in English, although Matt Reeck has done a translation that will hopefully be available soon. All translations in my discussion are my own.
2. Johnson, Erica L. "Building the Neo-Archive: Dionne Brand's *A Map to the Door of No Return.*" *Meridians* 12.1 (2014).
3. Here, I am also alluding to the title of her book of poetry, *Land to Light On.*

4. In Jean-Pierre Fournier's account, women were dispatched to French Guiana in its first decades, and marital unions were encouraged for a time but these led to a high number of abortions and deaths in childbirth; "En 1903, le gouvernement interrompis l'envoi de femmes en Guyane. L'idée de faire de cette contrée une colonie de peuplement avec l'aide de l'élément penal, était definitivement abandonée" (Fournier 26).

5. On the last point, see Michelle Alexander's *The New Jim Crow* and Ava DuVernay's documentary, *Thirteenth*.

6. Nora is quite forceful in his rhetorical opposition between history and memory; for example, "La mémoire est une phenomène toujours actuel, un lien vecu au present éternel; l'histoire, un representation du passé. Parce qu'elle est affective et magique, la mémoire ne s'accomode que de details qui la confortent" (Nora xix). In sum, Nora characterizes memory as affective, living, and organic whereas he sees history as a chronically incomplete and non-vital attempt to reconstruct and affix the past.

7. Andy Stafford helpfully contextualizes *Guyane* as a visual/textual genre among other such Francophone works. He points out that Chamoiseau has himself participated in other such projects (a visual text about Martinique for which he wrote captions, for example), and he looks at the way Hammadi and Chamoiseau participate in this larger genre. See his essay, "Patrick Chamoiseau and Rodolphe Hammadi in the Penal Colony. Photo Text and Memory Traces." *Postcolonial Studies* (January 11, 2008): 27–38.

8. I thank Carine Mardorossian for her commentary on this photo during my presentation of it at the 2017 NeMLA convention.

CHAPTER 4

Cultural Memory, Affect, and Countermonuments

Abstract This chapter addresses to role of public monuments and their role in the cultural memory of slavery in the United States Through a comparative analysis of the memorialization of slavery in the United States versus the Caribbean, and a historical look at monuments and race in the United States, the chapter concludes with a close reading of Kara Walker's 2014 monumental sugar sculpture, "*A Subtlety.*" A site-specific, temporary installation that no longer exists, the piece spoke to the dearth of monuments to the enslaved in the United States. By examining the sculpture's status as a countermonument, I present a full account of its reception and the violently varied feelings of viewers—feelings that live on as an affective archive of the topics it introduced into public space.

Keywords Countermonument · Race · Sugar · Slavery · Haunting · Pain

Toni Morrison alludes to the powerful affect of haunting in her seminal lecture, "Unspeakable Things Unspoken," in which she reflects at length on the erasure of African American presence from American literature and sums up the phenomenon thus: "the spectacularly interesting question is, What intellectual feats had to be performed by the author or his critic to erase me from a society seething with my presence" (Morrison 378), thereby positing a ghostly African American presence. As she says

© The Author(s) 2018
E. L. Johnson, *Cultural Memory, Memorials, and Reparative Writing*, Palgrave Studies in Affect Theory and Literary Criticism, https://doi.org/10.1007/978-3-030-02098-9_4

elsewhere in the same piece, "invisible things are not necessarily 'not-there'; a void may be empty, but is not a vacuum. In addition, certain absences are so stressed, so ornate, so planned, they call attention to themselves" (Morrison 378). Applying the same argument and logic to history, Morrison observed in a 1989 interview the dearth of memorials or commemorative sites in the United States to the transatlantic slave trade or to the nation's history of slavery, noting that there was not even "a small bench by the road" where she could sit and remember the lives of the enslaved. While there is still no federally funded monument in the nation's capital, the Toni Morrison Society did give the author a bench by the side of the road on Sullivan's Island, South Carolina, in 2008 and has added twenty more such benches around the United States and abroad since then. The point that Morrison raised goes even beyond that of whether memorial sites *exist* (although it is deeply significant that for the most part they do not exist in the United States), in that she makes note of the fact that it is not enough to just *know* about the most tragic chapter of U.S. history; one needs to *remember* it through the kind of memory work a memorial enables. Indeed, a memorial is designed to do just that: to introduce history into the viewer's cultural memory through feelings—typically feelings of loss, sorrow, and compassion but also potentially of shame, anger, and guilt. The bench by the side of the road is a site of convergence, where history and personal memory intertwine in a form of felt knowledge. This chapter takes up Morrison's point about the "stressed" and "ornate" absence of monuments commemorating enslaved people in the United States and examines the affective properties of public memorials and monuments. I conclude with an extended reading of Kara Walker's monumental sculpture, *A Subtlety, Or the Marvelous Sugar Baby* in which I show how the piece reflects upon the history of monumental art and how it produced an affective archive in the gaps of American cultural memory.

African American History in Monumental Art

Morrison's bench by the road provides a *lieu de mémoire*, which is a helpful concept for understanding why we need memorial art, and why the general refusal to represent African American history in such art is so consequential. In a collection entitled *History and Memory in African-American Culture*, the editors emphasize this idea as well as they seek "the retrieval of felt experience from the mix and jumble of the past" through the concept of the *lieu de mémoire*, which reconvenes "the polarization so often established between abstract, intellectual history and the affective stuff of memory" (Fabre and O'Meally 5, 7). By cinching together history and memory, which is precisely what a *lieu de mémoire* does, the editors and their contributors seek to empower "groups that until now have possessed reserves of memory but little or no historical capital" (McKay 284). McKay's point adds to our understanding of monuments that they, too, embody historical capital. While the notion of cultural currency plays out in the abstract forms of narrative and discourse, it is materially manifest in public monuments, and the fact that there are precious few such monuments to the history of slavery in the United States points to a gaping hole in national historical consciousness and to what can only be construed as willful amnesia on an epic scale. Caryl Phillips, who has written important, interventive fictions about the history of slavery, notes that:

> The reason it's important to have these memorials, these museums, these benches, is because it helps to stitch the present to the past… And so much of who we are as individuals or national groupings or racial or cultural groupings has been determined by this corner of history known as the slave trade and the African diaspora… The fact that it was hidden and ignored for many, many years has meant that there was work for writers and academics to do, and obviously other artists as well: photographers and painters and sculptors. (In Rice 2012, 366)

Phillips goes on in this 2012 interview to speculate that it is the next generation that will start to achieve a material recognition of this painful history, an insight that still seems apt if the 2017 removals of Confederate statues are to clear the way for a different form of cultural memory about antebellum U.S. history. While opponents to the statue removals bemoan the empty spaces they leave behind, no one seems yet to be talking about replacing monuments to white supremacy with markers to those who endured its violent rule. But the seething absence of memorials to centuries of the institution of slavery occupies those empty pedestals as surely as the stone and metal that stood there for most or all of the twentieth century. We can read in material signs the confrontation between memory and forgetting.

Moreover, the United States' particular practices of forgetting are all the more evident when we look at them in a comparative context with other parts of the Americas with which it shares a history in the slave trade. Like the United States, most Caribbean countries have their modern origins in slavery, conquered and established as they were by European powers as extensive plantations whose most important and influential agricultural product was sugar. However, in contrast to the dearth of monuments to that history in the United States, Caribbean islands are dotted with Emancipation Gardens, statues, monuments, and memorials commemorating the lives of those who suffered the curse of slavery and the many who revolted against it. To cite just a few examples, St. Croix features several statues including one of a man blowing a conch shell in a stance of revolution. There are also numerous examples of sculptural art featuring Maroons, a trope that provides a crucial counternarrative to that of victimization in that it commemorates the fact of ongoing resistance and the free communities of formerly enslaved people that formed throughout the islands and throughout the centuries. For example, in St. Martin there is a monument to a legendary one-breasted Maroon woman who strides toward her mountain, carrying firewood and a weapon. St. Martin also has a "Lady Liberty" statue of a tall and proud dark-skinned woman in a white gown who holds a lantern aloft to commemorate the end of slavery and, in a roundabout that every visitor sees as she leaves the airport on the Dutch St. Maarten side of the island, there is a large, strong statue of a man breaking his chains—a figure that appears prominently in Barbados as well.[1] Jamaica hosts a monument to Nanny of the Maroons, one of the most famous leaders of slave revolts in the Caribbean, and its Emancipation Garden features a large bronze sculpture commemorating a man and a woman standing for freedom. Martinique's Cap 110 is a powerful marker of the history of slavery with its fifteen bowed figures, weighing four tons each, facing out toward the Atlantic in the direction of Africa. While this is just a snapshot of the extensive memorialization that has taken place in the Caribbean, the point is that the trail to monumental art commemorating the enslaved has been blazed in this region adjacent to the United States while the vast landscape of the United States has remained relatively bare of such markers.

This is not to say that the United States is entirely without such monuments, but again a quick overview reveals its deficit of markers to the history of slavery. There is the African Burial Ground National Monument in lower Manhattan, which was dedicated in 2008 and which hosts an outdoor monument that commemorates the slave trade and asserts the role of African heritage in the United States The monument takes the form a large, abstract stone imprint of a ship's hull surrounded by global maps and sacred symbols of the many different religions practiced on the African continent.[2] The African Burial Ground monument might be counted as one of the more successful memorials, in light of the fact that attempts to represent African American history in monument form have sparked controversy as often as not.[3] To wit, Washington, DC does have a monument entitled The Freedman in a small park almost a mile from Capitol Hill. Designed by Edmonia Lewis, a sculptor of African American and Native American heritage, the monument was erected in 1863 and it became archetypal in its illustration of an emancipated slave kneeling in gratitude before a standing Abraham Lincoln. Such images proliferated in the forms of smaller statues and in paintings and illustrations, as Kirk Savage indicates in the very title of his book about Civil War monuments, *Standing Soldiers, Kneeling Slaves: Race, War, and Monument in Nineteenth-Century America*. While it is clearly problematic that the monument tells the story of emancipation as one enacted by a benevolent Lincoln, with no trace of African Americans' agency in their liberation or centuries of active resistance, The Freedman ushered in a symbolic order whereby the kneeling slave was later dropped from the image altogether and statues of Lincoln alone were taken to represent emancipation. Not to put too fine a point on it, but in this symbolic order black bodies were erased from the image of African American freedom altogether.

This is one of many trends in the representation of slavery—or the lack thereof—that Kirk Savage explores in his review of the classical history of sculpture in which he explains how the tradition eliminated black bodies in aesthetic as well as cultural terms. He writes, "African Americans loomed as the unspeakable reality that sculpture barely dared to approach... [because] the age-old status of the slave combined with the newer concept of race created an extremely powerful cultural formation that rendered the African American virtually the embodiment of what was *not* classically sculptural" (Savage 1999, 15). Savage's analysis provides a harsh indictment of the inability of white sculptors who were given commissions to represent "the people" to represent African Americans, whose bodies had found illustration only in the form of racist stereotype in paintings and drawings. With regard to sculpture, "African Americans could not simply be included in sculpture once slavery ended;

the very enterprise of sculpture would have to be reconstructed to make room for them and their history" (Savage 1999, 17).

One of the few monuments that did "make room for the black figures as concrete individual agents in the larger historical narrative they helped shape" (Savage 1999, 204) was Augustus Saint-Gaudens' *Shaw Memorial*, which was unveiled in Cambridge, Massachusetts in 1897. This memorial features prominently in Michelle Cliff's *Free Enterprise*, a novel in which she reconstructs the story of the historically marginalized figure of Mary Ellen Pleasant, an African American abolitionist and "a friend of John Brown," around several key works of art including the *Shaw Memorial* and J. M. W. Turner's painting of the infamous slave ship, *Zong*.[4] While Saint-Gaudens has been praised by art historians for basing his figures on real people, most of whom he encountered on the streets of New York, Cliff interrogates his use of stand-ins when he may have had access to photos of the real men who served as members of the 54th battalion, an African American unit of the Union Army led by General Shaw that perished in an unsuccessful raid on a Confederate fort. In either case, the memorial does break ground in sculptural representation of African Americans as individual men and not as types or caricatures, although the soldiers in the monument march beneath the figure of the white general that floats above them on his horse, thus maintaining the hierarchies of race within the rubric of military rank. Savage concludes that the explosion of sculptural public art that followed the Civil War ultimately "succeeded in prying apart the black body from the white nation" (Savage 1999, 222). At best, black bodies found representation but were still subverted, as was the case in the *Shaw Memorial* and at worst they were entirely excised from memorial art, as was the case with the solo Lincoln statues that were meant not only to represent the history of slavery, but to triumphantly close the door on it.

What is more troubling, the erasure and amnesia regarding African American history in the late nineteenth century, a period that Erika Doss identifies as a chapter in the nation's now-resurgent "memorial mania," was accompanied by the proliferation of representations of Confederate heroes and Ku Klux Klan leaders throughout the South— monuments that Americans are only now confronting. Doss points out that "in the decades following the Civil War, countless Confederate memorials were built in the United States" not only in the South, but in northern sites and indeed in the nation's capital, where "Arlington National Cemetery includes [an] audacious Confederate Monument, a thirty-two foot memorial decorated with a frieze of Greek gods and goddesses, handsome Confederate officers, and stoic slaves seeing their owners off to war" (Doss 11). Not only did such monuments proliferate in the period between 1870 and 1920 that Doss identifies as a phase of "memorial mania," but unlike the toppled statues of King George during the Revolutionary War and, in more recent cultural memory, the pulling down of statues of Saddam Hussein in the Iraq War, there was no national redress to symbols of the Confederacy. Instead, the monuments went up during the early years of the Jim Crow era to make a clear point about racial hierarchy, and they proliferated yet again during the Civil Rights Movement. These monuments were timed and designed specifically to assert white supremacy in moments when African Americans campaigned for equality. Writing in 2012, Doss observes that "the United States allows—or more accurately, ignores—memorials to the defeated states and underlying white supremacist politics of the secessionist Southern Confederacy" (Doss 10).

This reality may be changing as I speak, as I note in the introduction when I mention the 2017 removal of four monuments in New Orleans, three of which commemorated Confederate generals and the fourth a Reconstruction-era attack by white supremacists on an integrated police battalion. The removal of the monuments caused much relief and outcry. Their defenders expressed such outrage that the workers had to do their job at night wearing masks and bulletproof vests, as did those who removed Confederate monuments in Baltimore a couple of months later. In all of the debates and in the coverage of New Orleans Mayor Mitch Landrieu's decision to remove the statues, many argued that it is categorically important not to forget history, and that the monuments stood as reminders of the region's past, albeit a shameful one. What few remarked upon, though, was that those monuments stood in a city with no monuments at all to the black history upon which it is built. In the context of public memorialization, black history is *already* forgotten; the Confederate monuments stood not only as reminders of its regime, but they stood in fields of forgetting, on grounds of erasure.[5] Mayor Landrieu has been one of the very few people to speak to this point in his stirring speech about the monuments' removal:

> You see — New Orleans is truly a city of many nations, a melting pot, a bubbling caldron of many cultures. There is no other place quite like it in the world that so eloquently exemplifies the uniquely American motto: e

pluribus unum — out of many we are one. But there are also other truths about our city that we must confront. New Orleans was America's largest slave market: a port where hundreds of thousands of souls were bought, sold and shipped up the Mississippi River to lives of forced labor, of misery, of rape, of torture. America was the place where nearly 4000 of our fellow citizens were lynched, 540 alone in Louisiana; where the courts enshrined 'separate but equal'; where Freedom riders coming to New Orleans were beaten to a bloody pulp. So when people say to me that the monuments in question are history, well what I just described is real history as well, and it is the searing truth.

And it immediately begs the questions, why there are no slave ship monuments, no prominent markers on public land to remember the lynchings or the slave blocks; nothing to remember this long chapter of our lives; the pain, the sacrifice, the shame... all of it happening on the soil of New Orleans. So for those self-appointed defenders of history and the monuments, they are eerily silent on what amounts to this historical malfeasance, a lie by omission. There is a difference between remembrance of history and reverence of it. (Landrieu np)

New Orleans's monument removal is part of what appears to be a heightened attention to the powerful role that monumental art plays in defining national history and identity. The reason that universities, state legislatures, and town councils are struggling today with whether or not to remove statues, images, and names of slave-holders and advocates of slavery from their grounds is that so many such monuments were erected in a frenzied attempt to redefine the nation through public art after the Civil War and that they have not undergone scrutiny until very, very recently.[6] When Bree Newsome scaled a flagpole to remove the Confederate flag from South Carolina's capitol grounds in 2015 following the racially motivated murder of nine African American worshippers at a Charleston church, sparking the governor's decision to remove it indefinitely, she heightened many Americans' consciousness of the importance of such symbolism.[7] The widespread removal or plans for removal of Confederate monuments that followed the violence of neo-Nazi marchers in Charlottesville and Donald Trump's reprehensible refusal to condemn their violence in August of 2017, signals a sea change in national awareness of this issue.

Contemporary attempts to change our symbolic landscape stem less from knowledge about the past—most people living in the United States have some concept of the nation's history, however vaguely

and apologetically it may be taught in schools—but from the feelings of indignation, outrage, and insult that they inspire in their critics.
Confederate monuments stood as long as they did because, while many
people were certainly offended and pained by them, the majority of
Americans regarded them with emotional indifference. They became a
flashpoint when Mayor Landrieu recognized the hurt that they caused
his citizens, and when the Robert E. Lee memorial in Charlottesville
sparked feelings of pride and hatred in white supremacists. Memorials are
vessels of emotion: they are all about feelings, and the clash over them is
etched in shame, pride, and rage.

Even with this late-breaking conflict over Confederate memorials,
the impasse of nineteenth-century sculpture seems hardly to have been
remedied by twenty-first-century tactics. Whereas the nation is clearly
undergoing a shift in the conversation about how to represent its uglier
histories, this conversation has not achieved material representation, as a
quick overview of attempts to create public art to African American history reveals.

One case study of just how controversial and difficult it is to mount
a monument that deals with slavery is that of a proposed sculpture in
2011 in Indianapolis. The monument was to redress an existing sculpture's representation of an emancipated slave in a tableau of figures gath-
ered under an allegorical figure of Peace. The effort by the artist Fred
Wilson, who is African American, to recreate the figure from the existing *Soldiers and Sailors* Monument in a separate monument to pan-Af-
ricanism to be titled *E Pluribus Unum* is noteworthy for the fact that
the project was canceled before it could even be installed. As Modupe
Labode notes, "this... controversy turned on interpretations of the past,
particularly on what should be remembered and what should be forgotten about slavery" (Labode 1). Wilson proposed a piece that took the
slave figure from the 1902 monument and, preserving his seated and
reaching posture, positioned him holding a flag representing the African
Diaspora. In response, a group named Citizens Against the Slave Image
formed to protest the statue, arguing that any image of an enslaved person was a negative representation, and that any negative representation
of an African American added insult to existing injuries. Arthur Symes
said of another failed installation of public art representing black history, "The African American community has too many negatives, *real*
negatives, for those negatives to be emblazoned with pieces of artwork that will be there from now on. It would be a constant reminder"

(Finkelpearl 105).[8] As the name of the organization indicates, their argument was essentially that any depiction of a black person in allusion to slavery was negative, and upsetting; Bridget Cooks sums it up thus: "the group's concerns... were about wanting a *new* black image without reference to slavery and emancipation," although she also notes a certain acceptance of "the freedman's current invisibility in the Soldiers and Sailors Monument," which remained uncontested during the turmoil surrounding Wilson's work and stands in Indianapolis to this day (Cooks 29). Wilson's statue was never built, but its story illustrates the problem that "because we have so few representations of African Americans—and all people of color—in public art, initiatives for more representations are often embattled" (Cooks 31). And, again, the protests came from deep feelings of hurt that were much more powerful than the accompanying aesthetic and historical debates that took place.[9]

Cooks is not wrong in her point that almost any representation of African Americans has sparked controversy. Even Charles Keck's monument to Booker T. Washington on the Tuskegee University campus, *Lifting the Veil*, has been praised for its respectful embodiment of Washington and criticized for its reiteration of the Lincoln statues featuring kneeling slaves since it includes a strong-bodied man crouched and emerging from the veil Washington lifts. Keck, a white artist who worked as an assistant to Augustus Saint-Gaudens during the years that Saint-Gaudens created the *Shaw Memorial*, participated in the sculptural tradition of his mentor in this work of the 1930s. Another monument, in Savannah, depicting an African American family of a father, mother, son, and daughter was criticized for invoking the horrors of the Middle Passage in a written inscription and, simultaneously, for its ineffectiveness in commemorating African American history due to the seeming disconnect between its static nuclear family in modern clothing standing amidst broken chains. Designed by Dorothy Spradley, the monument also drew objections from those who saw the mere representation of slavery as a divisive move—a sentiment that corroborates the widespread desire to forget painful histories. Yet even for those who seek out cultural memory, Renée Ater argues, the memorial "disappoints because of the way the monument association, artist, and city officials have conflated historical and modern time, borrowed nineteenth-century conceits of freedom, and exploited early-twentieth-century ideas of racial uplift including the rhetoric of progress" (Ater 2010, 22).

Even the long-awaited arrival of a Dr. Martin Luther King, Jr. monument on the Washington Mall in 2011 has been cause for turmoil. The massive figure of King, standing with folded arms, his body only partially emergent from the wall of white granite from which he is cut, has been criticized for the whiteness of its material, the fact that a Chinese sculptor, Lei Yixin, was commissioned to make it and that he did so using Chinese materials and labor—and the attendant criticism that he made King's visage look vaguely Asian. Kevin Bruyneel reads the monument as a contributor to the untrue notion that the United States is a post-racial society in his observation that "the literally white King of the Stone of Hope reflects one way in which the haloed living myth gains popular appeal and serves as a powerful tool in politics when he is read as a man not defined by race, but by universal principles beyond or post-race. Here 'whiteness' is a universalizing signifier, not a racial identity or status" (Bruyneel 92–93). A truncated passage from one of King's speeches even had to be effaced from the monument after Maya Angelou pointed out that the paraphrase altered the meaning of the original passage for the worse.

This is not to say that all sculptures of African Americans are paradoxical, for there are successful and revered statues and monuments of Frederick Douglass and Harriet Tubman in multiple venues across the country. Douglass and Tubman do represent successful stories of resistance to slavery, and their monuments form important touchstones of African American history. There is also the Underground Railroad Memorial by sculptor Ed Dwight that stands on the shores of Detroit and Windsor, Ontario, spanning the river that so many crossed to reach freedom. Doss cites this memorial, with its eight life-sized figures of enslaved Americans achieving freedom as one of a few figurative works that "depict black slaves on heroic terms and slavery itself as a narrative of endurance and overcoming" (Doss 294).[10] She notes as well Ed Hamilton's Amistad Memorial in New Haven and his York, which commemorates the enslaved man who accompanied Lewis and Clark, in eight feet of bronze. Still, the comparative absence of black people from monuments and the absence of memorials to the traumatic history of slavery remains problematic. In New York City, for example, there are over a thousand public monuments, over three hundred of which are figural sculptures; twelve represent African American figures (including Douglass and Tubman). Moreover, existing monuments rarely attempt to represent the history of slavery in the United States, tuned in as they are to the triumphalist narrative that is taught in most US schools, as though the accomplishments of Civil Rights leaders and activists and the subsequent gains by African Americans spontaneously arose in the mid-twentieth century with no prior history of Jim Crow, the Civil War, slave revolts, or slavery itself. As Doss observes, "[freedom] remains the dominant trope in today's commemoration of slavery, and freedom frequently trumps slavery, against which it is pitted, not paired, in American historical memory" (Doss 293).

COUNTERMONUMENTS

A defining challenge of any attempted artistic representation of historical trauma in public art is that such works go against the tradition of memorials and monuments, erected as they are to mark criminals as well as victims, and to facilitate viewers' memories and knowledge of the past. Kirk Savage explains the challenges of monumentalizing painful histories in a Western sculptural tradition long dedicated to the celebration of allegorical figures and "great men," and he points out in *Monumental Wars* that the idea of creating "therapeutic" or "victim" memorials dates only as far back as the late twentieth century in the United States He cites Maya Lin's Vietnam memorial (1982) as the first therapeutic monument and the US Holocaust memorial museum, which opened in 1993, as the first victim memorial. Many art historians and cultural studies scholars have weighed in recently on the pressing questions about this new direction for monumental art. In the last twenty years or so, much has been written about how artists can or should create sites of commemoration of the Holocaust in particular, and there has been some attention to the commemoration of other dark chapters in history as well that often draws on the larger body of work on the Holocaust.[11] The Holocaust occupies a singular position in the field of cultural memory studies as perhaps the most thoroughly archived and recorded historical trauma and it is therefore taken as a frequent model for thinking through other histories. In any of these cases, though, the same questions arise: what are the ethics of representing historical trauma? What are the aesthetic imperatives of instilling an understanding of the past in individual viewers' memories? Monuments and memorials—and these terms are used interchangeably in critical discussions of such art—are imbued with more than just the task of representation; they are supposed to instill certain *feelings* in their viewers.[12] In the presence of a memorial, one is meant to not only remember the past, but to do so through a specific set of feelings that might include but are not limited to sorrow, pain, shame, appreciation, acknowledgement, and humility. As Erika Doss puts it, even the most conventional memorials "are archives of public affect, repositories of feelings and emotions that are embodied in their material form and content" (Doss 13).

Thus the ethical questions surrounding memorial and monumental art are couched in something of an affective mandate that pushes aesthetics in new directions. In contrast to sculptural traditions that represented "great men" fairly mimetically, monuments to loss, shame, guilt, and suffering, have of necessity explored new forms of representation. It is one thing if a monument is designed to celebrate an individual and quite another if it is to signify loss of life and suffering on a large scale. These two monumental projects raise different aesthetic and ethical questions. For example, whereas the Lincoln Memorial in Washington, DC with its enormous, seated form of Lincoln, is widely embraced as a worthy tribute to a towering figure in American history, a figural representation of a mass historical trauma has a different relationship to the human form. Richard Crownshaw says of such memorials, with regard to the Holocaust, "remembrance risks paralleling the sacrificial logic of anti-Semitism, turning victims remembered into a sacrificial object in the restoration of a national identity" (Crownshaw 204). Crownshaw implies that the depiction of victims' bodies would mask individuals' suffering in abstraction, and risk reducing victims to materials for artists' ambitions and for public consumption. For this reason a fair amount of post-World War II memorial art has pushed into the field of non-figural abstraction, whether we are speaking of Holocaust memorials like the hundreds of stone slabs laid out in remembrance in Berlin, the Vietnam Memorial wall, the stone chairs that memorialize those killed in the Oklahoma City bombings, the bottomless, cascading fountains of the 9/11 memorial in New York, or the ruined ship that forms a memorial to the Great Famine in Ireland and the symbolic ruins that commemorate the same history in New York.

That said, there remains a larger question of excising bodies from such monuments given that black, Jewish, female, Roma and disabled bodies, among others, had already been rendered absent from monuments by sculptural tradition and practices. The double exclusion of bodies that had never been represented in the tradition of figural sculpture in the first place is troubling. Are efforts to render suffering in only abstract images complicit with an original erasure from figural art? What is the place of the body in memorial art that does not celebrate particular bodies but, rather, commemorates bodily suffering and mental anguish? These questions point to the need for such monuments to reconfigure the field of representation in a way that challenges the history of monumental art designed to serve ruling powers, nation-states, and hegemonic worldviews in aesthetic terms that defy conventional forms.

Whether figural and mimetic or abstract, though, in contrast to monuments designed to offer some kind of conclusion about and hence closure on a life or a historical event, memorials to trauma exceed their material boundaries to take up residence in viewers' feelings about the past and the "postmemories" those feelings evoke, to use Marianne Hirsch's term. Hirsch defines postmemory as the phenomenon through which history persists in a transgenerational form, whether within the context of familial or social generations. Whereas individuals' memories of their own experiences are mediated in large part by recall, postmemories are accessible only through channels of affect and intellectual commitment; "Postmemory's connection to the past is thus not actually mediated by recall but by imaginative investment, projection, and creation... these events happened in the past, but their effects continue into the present" (Hirsch 107). In the case of Holocaust memorials, Crownshaw argues that such works prompt viewers to not only gaze and reflect upon a material site, but to do a certain kind of post/memory work that transforms the viewer into a "proxy" witness "through the staging of an empathetic identification with Holocaust witnesses and something approximating the remembrance of their experiences from their point of view" (Crownshaw vi). The centrality of the viewer's felt remembrance of the past makes a memorial's affective dimensions its most essential.

In light of the impossibilities and pitfalls of representation in the memorials he studies, Crownshaw suggests that the more successful works go so strongly against the tradition of celebratory and commemorative monuments as to become "countermonuments." The artists and architects of the monuments he examines work with affect as though it were a raw material. Because a monolithic version of the past is impossible in the face of trauma, artists turn to countermonumental forms and spaces that focus more on *feelings* than on *narratives* about the past. Countermonuments, he argues, convey "the rupture or wound as [victims] were torn from the social and cultural fabric   The consequent incompleteness of these monuments—their architectural articulation of the wound and their refusal to complete the representation of those they remember—creates space for the visitors' continuation of the memory work that cannot be concluded by the monument" (Crownshaw 186). The countermonument, then, could take any number of representative forms but its most important quality is that it "foregrounds the highly mediated nature of such cultural memory work [and] encourages in the visitor a highly self-reflexive relationship to the past and to the remembrance of the past" (Crownshaw186). It is the shift in emphasis from the object of the monument as a representational form to the affective impact of its many qualities on the viewer that makes a work a countermonument. The idea of the countermonument thus provides a helpful answer to questions I have raised about the ethics and aesthetics of commemorating trauma in that its primary function is to activate the viewer's felt knowledge about the past and its ongoing presence in contemporary life.

Countermonumental art could address problems associated with the representation of African American history in public art and monuments in the United States A countermonument can capture *forgetting*, and even absence. Such an artistic endpoint embodies the paradox of American memorial sculpture, and it is the direction in which I want to head in my approach to Kara Walker's sculpture. More specifically, I am interested in the temporal as well as affective dimensions of some countermonuments, which Michael Rothberg notes (in terms that echo Chamoiseau's comments about monuments in chapter two): "While traditional monuments are supposed to be stable, timeless, 'monumental,' and aesthetically pleasing, countermonuments are often *dynamic, temporary, fleeting*, and deliberately unaesthetic" (Rothberg 469, emphasis mine).

The fleeting temporality of many countermonuments is germane to Walker's piece and to a couple of other countermonuments that explore the same history that she does. One of the most interesting and complicated countermonuments to fit this description is the Middle Passage Monument, built in St. Croix and transported to New York in 1998. An abstract piece by sculptor Eddie Dixon, it is composed of two stone arches and was unveiled in a funereal ceremony, hauled onto a replica of a slave ship, dispatched out to sea, and then lowered to the floor of the Atlantic Ocean. Although a reproduction of the piece stands in St. Croix, the original work, now absent from view, resides only in affective archives; "it offers no consolation in a public space in the city and it cannot serve as a gathering place for commemorative activity there. The burden of remembering rests with those women and men who witnessed the dedication ceremony or the lowering of the monument and those who continue to read about it" (Ater 2010, 21). Renée Ater sees this monument as an effective response to the "'unsettling memory' [of slavery] which can evoke feelings of shame and antipathy in public monuments" and which, because so anguished, can "encourage us to forget it, yet, it is deeply woven into the fabric of who we are as a nation" (Ater 2010, 20). Similarly, there is an underwater sculpture located off the coast of Grenada by Jason de Caires Taylor entitled *Vicissitudes* which, while more accessible than The Middle Passage Monument in that divers can view it, plays with the notion of temporality in its submersion. *Vicissitudes* is composed of a circle of women and men holding hands on the ocean floor. As Fred Wilson writes, "The first time I saw it on the internet I, like many others, immediately saw it as an incredible expression of the horrors of the Middle Passage... I viewed the sculpture as an evocation of the souls of these folks in the waters of the Caribbean" (Wilson 11).[13] As Wilson notes, these disappeared monuments can continue to provoke feelings even in those who cannot view them, yet their temporary status on land is significant. By creating material monuments and then removing them from the status of public art, the artists create countermonuments that represent the *absence* of monuments commemorating the Middle Passage even while they leave a powerful affective residue. They illustrate the impact that fleeting, temporary sculptures have in raising the specters of the past in such a way that they offer no closure but rather keep open the door to what they represent. As James Young says of Hamburg's Monument Against Fascism, a twelve-foot tall pillar that slowly sank into the ground over a period of years until it disappeared, "How better to remember forever a vanished people than by the perpetual unfinished, ever-vanishing monument?" (Young 31). Young sees the interred pillar as a countermonument in its "brazen, painfully self-conscious memorial space conceived to challenge the very presence of [its] being" (Young 27). The fact that one cannot visit, reflect upon, and then walk away from these monuments means that they reside in a more open-ended and affective state of meaning.

The countermonument is thus anything but cathartic. While much memorial public art is designed precisely to close off the past, countermonuments stir it up in the hearts and minds of their viewers. As the authors of a piece on "Feminist Memorializing and Counter-Memory" argue, "if hegemonic memorializing is often about active forgetting—individualizing and remembering on behalf of communities—countermemorializing needs to promote active remembering... which involves communities taking responsibility for the systemic nature of gendered violence" (Bold, Knowles, and Leach 130). I would point out that the kind of memory that we are talking about here is in equal parts memory and haunting when haunting refers to that material from the past that cannot be remembered and held in the mind, nor can it be assimilated into narrative. In fact, Marisa Parham describes haunting in much the same way that others discuss postmemory: "Being haunted means struggling with things that come to us from outside our discreet experiences of the world, but which we nevertheless experience as emerging from our own psyches" (Parham 436). Such material can be processed into a form of knowledge only through feelings, whether these feelings are disturbing, uncomfortable, confusing, inexplicable, or even nostalgic. Moreover, hauntings cannot be closed off or concluded; through flows of affect, they ensnare the mind and body in whatever is unsettled about the past. Avery Gordon emphasizes as well the role of affect in her analysis of haunting as "a social phenomenon of great import" (Gordon 7); she observes that "being haunted draws us affectively, sometime against our will and always a bit magically, into the structure of feeling of a reality we come to experience, not as cold knowledge, but as a transformative recognition" (Gordon 8). Hegemonic memorials are designed to enable memory by stirring up feelings on site in such a way that one can then walk away and forget; they are less attuned to hauntings than countermonuments, which take up residence in the viewer so that the feelings they elicit are borne away by the viewer, internally. Thus, I would argue that the primary effect of a countermonument is that it imbues viewers with not only a sense of witnessing, but with an ongoing sense of being haunted by the material one has absorbed in the presence of the monument. The intertwined thoughts and feelings provoked by an encounter with countermonumental art can effect a new role of the past in the social present; it can effect an affective archive of shared if deeply unsettling histories.

The Affective Archive of *A Subtlety*

I now turn to a case study that throws into relief the many issues I have raised in this chapter, from Morrison's critique of absent memorials to the question of whose bodies figure in monumental art to that of the function of countermonuments. The subject of this case study is Kara Walker's enormous art installation in the ruins of the Domino sugar refinery in Brooklyn in 2014. This sculpture, entitled *A Subtlety, or The Marvelous Sugar Baby*, presided over some 100,000 viewers from all over New York City and all over the world during that summer in the doomed sugar factory on the Brooklyn waterfront. The Domino sugar plant, built in 1856, was for a time the largest sugar processing factory in the world; by the late nineteenth century it processed over half of the sugar consumed in the United States. This massive operation came to a slow in the late twentieth century and a halt in the early twenty-first, and it was subsequently scheduled for demolition in order to make way for luxury condos. Before the site was transitioned from derelict ruins into shiny new housing units, though, it became a temporary gallery for a work of art meant to speak to its history in some way. Walker was commissioned by the arts organization Creative Time to create such a work of public art and her response was *A Subtlety*.

Rarely have critical reactions varied so widely or so powerfully (except perhaps in some of the cases I've already highlighted). This is true of Walker's entire career, though. When she became the youngest person ever granted a MacArthur "genius grant" at the age of 27, other artists—predominantly African American artists—immediately formed a petition to have the honor revoked on the basis that her artwork was deeply offensive in its use of racial stereotype, caricature, and sexually graphic and abasing images. The stereotypes and caricatures in which she traffics are products of the white racist imagination, and a lineage of such representations can be traced back to the noxious images of such nineteenth-century British animators as George Cruikshank, James, Gillray, and Richard Newton, whose popular representations of Africans and African Americans established influential stereotypes and visual slurs. Cruikshank illustrated Harriet Beecher Stowe's *Uncle Tom's Cabin* among other things, and his work along with that of his colleagues appeared often in the popular press. Even their work for abolitionist venues, though, provides fodder for Walker in her engagement with historical visual racial slurs. Their aesthetic established the trope of exaggerated bodily features, and they approached the black body as "the site for terrible anxieties and repressions involving white sexual confusion and guilt about the slave trade" (Wood 161). It is this history and aesthetic with which Walker engages in her work—which is to say that she confronts the historical white imagination in her art. As a representation of the ugliness of racist conceptualizations of the body, Walker's pieces work as devastating revelations and critiques. As representations of black bodies, identities, or experience, though, they are betrayals. The problem is that it is almost impossible to parse the searing exposure of the centuries-long formation of white racist psyches from the damage they have and continue to wreak. In a *Village Voice* article about Walker's 2017 exhibit in New York, Siddharta Mitta observes that, "Like the revolutionary psychiatrist Frantz Fanon, who treated both torturers and the tortured during the Algerian War, Walker knows that oppression degrades victim and perpetrator alike; her work explores, in the American setting, this terrain" and he adds that "She references not just antebellum life but the continuum of Black freedom dreams denied by white psychosis" (Mitta np). Walker's images may expose and damn the sickness of the white psyche, but they stage this critique upon black wounds and cause profound pain. And the feelings that Walker stirs up when she pulls back the curtain on the racist imaginary are, as Clyde Taylor puts it, "non-negotiable."

The paradox of Walker's work is evident in a collection of essays about her silhouette and film art that preceded her sugar sculpture. Entitled *Kara Walker-No/ Kara Walker-Yes/ Kara Walker-?*, the volume gathers pieces by numerous black artists and intellectuals who weigh in on her work. The vast majority of the contributors finds her art deplorable and they explain her success as an appeal to white audiences who, they charge, take pleasure in viewing debasing images of black characters in her silhouettes. While this discussion of Walker's public art in the Domino factory does not seek to engage her earlier work, the collection of essays illustrates Walker's ability to create affective distress through her corpus: Howard McCalebb refers in his essay to a state of "apoplexy" that surrounds her art, and other writers express outrage, hurt, grief, humiliation, shame, rage, disgust, horror, and any number of other negative feelings in very strong and clear terms. (The brief excerpts in the "Kara Walker-Yes" section take up only a sliver of the book, and the similarly concise "Kara Walker-?" section expresses profound ambivalence.) The editor, Howardena Pindell, notes that the same works that garnered such harsh criticism among most of the contributors had also received glowing praise in reviews in mainstream media and in the white-dominated art world, and her collection illustrates a contrast between impassioned critiques by black artists and intellectuals alongside detached, laudatory essays by white critics.

As Kim Wickham says of Walker's notorious silhouettes, Walker not only divides critics, but this division should prompt critics to "interpret interpretations," to put positive and negative reviews into dialogue with one another in order to understand why Walker "elicit[s] such visceral reaction in the viewer"; she goes on to say that "it is the experience of the viewer, the disorientation, disgust, investment, fascination that is what is at stake in Walker's work" (Wickham 336). Disorientation, disgust, investment, fascination? Such feelings seem anathema to the feelings of humility, grief, and honor that monuments to the past are supposed to elicit, yet there is no question that the sphinx, as Walker called her sugar sculpture, provoked many negative feelings along with those seemingly more compatible with memorial art. That said, the sheer power of the responses to Walker's sculpture has stirred up an affective archive of feelings about not only the history of sugar, slavery, racism, and sexism, but the ongoing imprint of these histories on contemporary culture. These feelings exceed the individual, playing out as they did in a public space. As Teresa Brennan defines "the transmission of affect," "affects have an energetic dimension. That is why they can enhance or deplete... we are not self-contained in terms of our energies. There is no secure distinction between the 'individual' and the 'environment'" (Brennan 6).

MEMORIALIZING SUGAR

For anyone familiar with the history of sugar, as Walker was, the project of representing its role in global agriculture, industry, and trade would pose a grim assignment indeed. Arguably the scourge of the New World, the sugar industry relied on and perpetuated slave and indentured labor throughout the Americas for centuries and was a driving force of the Triangle Trade during the seventeenth and eighteenth centuries and the domestic slave trades that continued thereafter. The process of harvesting sugar cane was particularly brutal: it grows in extreme heat, its tall canes are difficult to cut and sharp and splintery once they are, and the processing of sugar involved grueling mills and suffocating temperatures as the stalks were boiled down into molasses and then refined into white sugar or fermented into rum. Sidney Mintz chronicles the particular dangers and pressures of sugar production in the Caribbean in *Sweetness and Power*, in which he notes that the process was driven not only by profit and demand, but by "the somewhat misleading idea that sugar syrup, once boiling, should not be permitted to cool until 'struck'" with the result that the "men and women in the factory worked continuously in shifts lasting all day and part of the night, or the whole of every second or third night" in "heat and noise [that] were overpowering" and in conditions of "considerable danger" (Mintz 49). Of course, this process had become automated in the twentieth century to reduce the human labors and perils that founded the industry, but the task of representing the sugar industry is inevitably entangled with slavery and suffering, as Walker, who has referred to the industry as "blood sugar," understood her task. Mintz's capacious history recounts as well the thirty-year period in the early nineteenth century during which sugar consumption in Britain increased by 500 percent, and he notes that by the twentieth century, "sugar is so familiar, so common, and so ubiquitous that it is difficult to imagine a world without it" (Mintz 74)—and indeed we continue to live in an era when, so universal is sugar, that "campaigns are waged against it" (Mintz 74). The ubiquity of the product today further obscures its human legacy of violence, suffering, and death in cane fields, mills, and refineries.

While few viewers or critics construed Walker's public sculpture as either monument or memorial, there is no question that her 40,000-ton, thirty-five foot-tall sugar sculpture of a naked, caricatured black woman crouched in the pose of the sphinx and clenching her left fist in a sign of insult, spoke to the history of slavery, exploitation, and physical and psychic violence incurred by the sugar industry. Similarly, the dozen or so four-foot tall "molasses boys" that surrounded her were figures of barely clad, barefoot children doing the labor of hauling fruit in baskets or in their hands. Ephemeral in their construction, many of the molasses boys melted and broke apart during the exhibit while the sphinx powdered away; there are a few resin replicas of the child figures in museums such as the Brooklyn Museum and MoMA, but the original figures collapsed and the sphinx was dismantled after the exhibit and no longer exists in material form. For several weeks, though, all of these statues stood as a rare expression of a largely repressed history as though they erupted from the forgetfulness surrounding an industry that has only grown exponentially since its criminal origins, and one that we continue to take into our bodies at an alarming and damaging rate. Walker explained that the statue "was talking about slavery, race, submission, women's bodies, our history—but withholding that language. It's incumbent on the viewer," she said, "to bring that language forward" (Walker NYPL interview). Indeed, her statue's allusion to her sister sphinx in Egypt makes her an interlocutor, a figure whose viewers are tasked with answering the riddles she poses.

In discussions of her work, Walker classifies her statue as "public art" and as "monumental art," and she speaks of her attempts to create a "reverent" space.[14] This framing of the piece suggests that it holds monumental properties, but in contrast to monuments designed to fix a historical narrative in bronze or stone, Walker's ephemeral sugar sculpture did not endure as an object but rather as an affective space in its viewers, and it thus pushes back against the non/history of national monuments and memorials surrounding the history of slavery in the United States to form a uniquely affective monumental event. By placing viewers in the literal shadow of sugar, Walker provoked feelings about history's weight upon the present, and by placing them in the sickly sweet, rancid odors of the factory, she ushered viewers into the affective space of labor. While the artist's intentions cannot hold sway over interpretations of her art, as we will see in the painfully varied reactions to Walker's sculpture, her goal of forcing viewers to enact their own emotions and language was irrefutably effective as well as affective.

While the sculpture was certainly monumental, it was also countermonumental in the sense that it was temporary and has now disappeared from sight, much like the Middle Passage Monument that now sits on the floor of the Atlantic and the sinking column in Hamburg. In fact, Walker goes a step further in that, unlike the interred column or the sunken sculpture, Walker's sphinx no longer exists. She leaves only affective traces in memory, in images, and in writing. Furthermore, another noteworthy aspect of the sculpture is that it is a figural countermonument. Most works that have been construed as countermonuments are abstract. However, *A Subtlety* was a forceful embodiment that compares to a massive figural sculpture in Guyana by Philip Moore, *1762 Monument*, that commemorates a slave revolt in the form of a massive stone figure representing "Cuffy," the leader of the revolt. The insistence on embodiment, which is visible in any number of Caribbean monuments of smaller scale, enters into a tradition of non-representation of black bodies; as Marcus Wood demonstrates, even abolitionist tracts in the nineteenth century tended to either eliminate figural rep-resentation or to present "erotically charged" bodies. That said, both the Cuffy monument and *A Subtlety* are erotically charged, with Cuffy holding phallic weapons in his hands and the sphinx's colossal nudity and exaggerated breasts and vulva. Walker's mimicry—in the classical sense of imitating and mocking—of a long tradition of such representation prompted complex and conflicting feelings in her viewers.

The affective archive of the piece exists in writing as well as in the lived experience of visitors who physically shared presence with the sphinx and one another. It is therefore important to take a look at the divergent reviews of *A Subtlety*, which form one dimension of the affective archive given how many of the critical responses are written in a vocabulary that is emotional as well as intellectual. The emotional timbre of many of the pieces written about *A Subtlety* makes them an introductory catalog of the feelings that surrounded it. The mainstream press overwhelmingly praised the installation, with *The Huffington Post* putting it at the top of a list of the fifteen most important pieces of art of 2014. The senior art critic for *The New York Times*, Roberta Smith, lauded the piece as "a power image, a colossal goddess of the future awaiting veneration. With blank eyes, she might also be a blind diviner" of America's future. Smith describes the sphinx as "beautiful, brazen, and disturbing." While she does focus primarily on the inde-terminacy of the sphinx's meaning—"above all [it is] a densely layered statement that both indicts and pays tribute. It all but throws possible interpretations and inescapable meanings at you… [as] a grand, decay-ing structure fraught with the conflicted history of the sugar trade and its physical residue"—there is no question that her review is overall an appreciative one. Smith evokes the work's "power" no fewer than three times. Writing for *The New Yorker*, Hilton Als called the piece "trium-phant, rising from another kind of half world—the shadowy half world of slavery and degradation as she gives us a version of 'the finger'" (Als np). Whereas Smith sees ambiguity and ambivalence in what Walker is doing with race, Als sees a robust critique of the haunting racism that the statue manifests: "Walker knows that ghosts can hurt you because history does not go away. Americans live, still, in an atmosphere of phantasmagori-cal genocide—we kill each other with looks, judgments, the fantasies that white is better than black and that blackness is bestial while being somehow more 'humane'—read mentally inferior—than whiteness" (Als np). While he performs a classical reading of the sphinx in the con-text of Western art history and its "radical" refiguration of the female body, Als's reference to the pain of history and its transmutation into affective "genocide" in the present reflects the emotional medium of Walker's critique.

Given that many of the sphinx's features were direct manifestations of the racist imagination, Als and Francey Russell both argue that that racism demands to be read; Russell writes, "She is a site of contest between racist and non-racist conceptualizations of power and personhood, representing a whole host of European-American projections, associations, and history: now a strong woman, now a mammy, now a sexualized body, now an animalized body, now a sphinx" (Russell np). Russell describes *A Subtlety* as "an emotional and serious work" that "commands the space in a new and startling way" (Russell np). She too offers an overall positive review of *A Subtlety* in which she focuses on the problems of spectatorship and seeing that stemmed from the exhibition—an issue that is problematic precisely because the spectatorship was so splintered. And, as Kristen West Savali explains, even individual viewers' feelings were splintered internally. She describes her own responses to the sculpture, which she approached as a figment of hurtful "mammy" iconography, thus: "Rarely has art triggered so many feelings in me: anger, sadness, fear, empathy, protectiveness, pride, joy. Love. It is haunting, powerful, captivating" (Savali np). In another comment on the emotionally capacious provocations of the piece, Hank Willis Thomas hazards an assessment of how it *should* make viewers feel: "You're supposed to feel drawn in and horrified by the work. For me the sphinx does that. She can make something repulsive and beautiful and sticky and troublesome all at the same time" (Thomas np). Thomas's comment points to a problem, though, which is precisely that whatever the artist intended or whatever one is *supposed* to feel, viewers brought so many different personal histories, and such a differentiated set of interpretive tools to the Domino factory that what unspooled was more like affective anarchy. Even the largely appreciative critical responses, which register feelings of humility or discomfort before the sphinx's frequently mentioned "power," also register hurt, shock, and the gamut of emotions that Savali names.

If the positive reviews contained negative feelings, the negative reviews were scathing, as we see in a special issue of *Black Renaissance Noire* dedicated to *A Subtlety*. Contributors to this issue condemn Walker for everything from reinforcing racism, to perpetuating child and forced labor in her use of sugar, to environmental corruption in her use of polystyrene (which formed the internal frame of the sphinx), to foisting her own feelings of self-loathing on her audience. Carol Diehl argues,

"That Walker's work is celebrated, even tolerated, tells us a lot about the racism that is still subtly endemic to the art world" (Diehl 94), and she accuses Walker of advertising the product of a particularly corrupt and exploitative sugar plantation in the Dominican Republic where much of the sugar that went into the sculpture was cultivated. Paul Carter Harrison responds to Henry Louis Gates, Jr.'s assessment that the statue performed a critique of racist imagery with the charge that, rather, it reiterated and reified the very racism it was supposed to critique. He pointedly muses, "I wonder what story would be represented for the American public if a favorite icon like The Statue of Liberty were replicated as a nude, 2-story tall sensuous Siren of the Sea" in a lewd posture (Harrison 101). The conversation is deeply polarized, with the convener of the issue, Clyde Taylor, defending aspects of Walker's art while his colleagues for the most part attack it. Brenda Marie Osbey speaks for many when she says that while Walker may be playful about the tropes she engages and even about her own anxieties, "it's important to remember, however, that the self-hatred typical of most if not all of Walker's work is not personal. It extends to all of us" (Osbey 96). Ultimately, Taylor concludes that "Everyone brings feelings and experiences to a work of art, and among Black people these can include deep hurts and tender, sacred, non-negotiable spaces" (Taylor 93), as the writers who expressed their own feelings of hurt and outrage in the issue demonstrate. Taylor's observation points to the fact that the affective impact of Walker's installation was so great that viewers' feelings deeply informed and were informed by their interpretations of the representational schema of the monumental body and her small attending statues. Between the positive and negative reviews, there was intense emotional engagement with the work during the exhibit that continues to reverberate in its absence.

This is so precisely because the "non-negotiable spaces" to which Taylor refers are affective spaces, the spaces where the sphinx took up residence during her reign and the spaces where she currently resides. As Taylor notes elsewhere, the absent status of the disappeared statue puts anyone writing about it in the position of writing about an object that exists only in memory and as a ghost: "Writing more about what I saw and reacted to—a one-off, site-specific construction—would be like dissecting a phantom" (Taylor 93). Indeed, the absent sphinx exists *only* in memory, individual and cultural, and in the hauntings and other affective traces she left—and she left a massive tangle of affective traces. Indeed, one criticism of the installation that came from various sides was precisely that it invited such a range of affective response in its framing—or lack thereof. That is, Walker could have contextualized her figures in information that mapped out the enmeshed trade routes of sugar and human beings, or statistics about the consumption of sugar and the pace of the slave trade, or about the horrific labor conditions in which the industry has its origins—or even statistics about how sugar consumption has resulted in a contemporary diabetes epidemic that in the United States disproportionally affects African Americans. Instead, she provided only a cryptic statement, painted on the outer wall of the factory that read: "A Subtlety or the Marvelous Sugar Baby, an Homage to the unpaid and overworked Artisans who have refined our Sweet tastes from the cane fields to the kitchens of the New World on the Occasion of the demolition of the Domino Sugar Refining Plant." While the term "homage" could indicate the memorial nature of the sculpture and the word "unpaid" alludes to enslaved and indentured labor, the rhetorical framework for *A Subtlety* is by far its most subtle dimension.

Viewers, who had first to stand in a line nearly a mile long, saw only this enigmatic and often overlooked introduction before signing a waiver and entering the factory, where they breathed in the sickly sweet odor of rancid syrup, felt stickiness under their feet, encountered the palpable layers of liquid sugar and molasses that had dripped down the walls for well over a century, and saw the sphinx rising at the far end of the space. The viewing experience was thus profoundly sensual, whether in terms of the strong smell, the granular texture underfoot, and the heat of the space, or in terms of the experience of feeling and witnessing others' feelings of respect, revulsion, grief, glib curiosity, awe, or anger. The viewing experience was also inherently social since the dissonant responses of the audience were inseparable from a visit to the site and thus to anyone's account of the sculpture. As the poet Claudia Rankine, who found her visit to be "exhausting" observed, "If you can't or won't do the math, then the space must hold your reactions too" (in Berlant 2014). Rankine's comment corroborates Brennan's point that affects are transmitted in "a process that is social in origin but biological and physical in effect... the emotions or defects of one person, and the enhancing of depressing energies these affects entail, can enter into one another" (Brennan 3). Because there was no provision of a narrative for viewers, no contextual instruction, visitors brought varying degrees of ignorance and knowledge of Domino and the sugar industry to the project. Walker's refusal to instruct her viewers about how to understand the racialized and sexualized figure that stood over them meant that some saw the racism and sexism as damning products of slavery and sugar, others saw pure racism and sexism without critique, and still others saw nothing but spectacle and even titillation. Incredibly, the sinister history that gave rise to the "mammy" caricature towering over them in tons of sugar was invisible to many visitors; apparently, the entire brutal story of sugar needed to be spoon-fed to some. Whereas some saw an ethical lapse in Walker's withholding of contextual information, Valerie Loichot argues that the sculpture, true to her allusion to the Egyptian Sphinx, "demands an ethical response," one that is the responsibility of the viewer, not the artist.

The narrative ambiguity of the piece fed tremendous affective distress not only because viewers had different reactions, but because those different feelings were manifest, as Rankine notes, *in the same space.* Humbled viewers and deeply offended and hurt viewers comingled with viewers who brought no historical interest to the statue at all and treated her as nothing more than a crude selfie-op. Walker surreptitiously filmed the audience and put together a short video that she posted on YouTube, in which you see small children dipping their hands in pools of molasses and viewers of all backgrounds and nationalities responding with smiles and laughter or with great sobriety. The worst offenders/provocateurs were those who jeered or took lewd photos of the breasts and vulva.[15] A common and obviously offensive pose was that where viewers stood in front of the sphinx's breasts as though they were tweaking her nipples, and there were any number of insensitive and crude photos taken of her posterior. Walker herself said,

> I put a ten-foot vagina in the world and people respond to ten-foot vaginas in the way that they do. It's not unexpected. Maybe I'm sick. Sometimes I get a sort of kick out of the hyper essay writing, that there's gotta be this way to sort of control human behavior. [But] human behavior is so mucky and violent and messed-up and inappropriate. And I think my work draws on that. It comes from there. It comes from responding to situations like that and it pulls it out of an audience. I've got a lot of video footage of that behavior. I was spying.[16]

The responses that Walker and others recorded in photos, videos, and social media postings provide evidence of how impoverished cultural memory surrounding the history of sugar, the history of slavery, and the history of the Americas is for Americans and international tourists alike.

In social media, where much of the affective effect of the sphinx lives on, a viewer named Stephanye Watts described the interruption of her own feelings of grief by a white male viewer's contempt and boredom, which prompted her to pose the incredulous question, "How do you not realize that you are currently standing on sacred ground and staring the sickness of our country dead in the face?"[17] In this encounter, Watts absorbed her own reactions, which she describes elsewhere in her post as those of reverence and appreciation for black women's suffering, as well as the reactions of the callous man next to her—a reaction that could be classified as a uniquely "ugly feeling" that Sianne Ngai explores in her book of the same name. That is, the man expresses his sense of "stuplimity," a feeling that Ngai defines as "a strange amalgamation of shock and boredom," for his emotional journey after the "wow" moment of encounter was to dullness. Because affects are not just internal but rather are social and flow between objects and people, Watts was contaminated by the man's ugly feelings. This transmission of affect meant that, while she ideally wanted to think about her own connectedness to her ancestors' past, she had to sit simultaneously with the erasure of that past in the cultural memory of another spectator. The sphinx's form thus embodied both history and the erosion of historical memory in her disintegrating presence.

One thing that almost all viewers did, whatever their reaction, was to take photos. This now universal reaction to spectacle united viewers in the sense that everyone stood in the same pose with their phone or camera at one point, and in the sense that everyone's photos contained each other as they snapped shots amidst dense crowds. Audience members' bodies flowed into one another's photos as their feelings flowed into one another's responses. Walker has pointed to another problem with not only the tacky selfies, but the entire practice of picture taking surrounding *A Subtlety*. Whether the photos were taken voyeuristically, narcissistically, or respectfully, they sought exactly the kind of closure that her work eschews. Along with the written accounts of the installation, these photos now comprise the sphinx's archive in her absence.

In this we see Walker making a move away from conventional monumental art, designed as it is to enable "closure" on negative feelings. In their photo taking, Walker saw viewers trying to "manage the unmanageable" (NYPL interview). As a countermonument, though, the sphinx's meaning bled out into feelings that filled the absence of narrative and of fixity. Brian Massumi, in his influential "The Autonomy of Affect," explains that affective responses to the world are unmediated by narrative yet deeply embedded in memory, configured as memory is by "intensi-ties." He writes that, in contrast to conscious narratives of meaning, affective intensities are "outside expectation and adaptation, as discon-nected from meaningful sequencing, from narration, as from vital func-tion. It is narratively de-localized, spreading over the generalized body surface, like a literal backwash from the function—meaning interloops traveling the vertical path between head and heart" (Massumi 85)—and, in another evocative phrase, Massumi points out that "the skin is faster than the word." This means that even those viewers who were ignorant of historical narrative produced affective material not only within them-selves but among co-audience members, for the residue of one person's affects looped into those of others in the space of the installation. In the example of Watts's account, the sphinx produced one man's boredom beside her own feelings of reverence, feelings that reveal more than dif-ferent appraisals of art: they reveal the extent to which the history of slav-ery is forgotten or repressed in his case, or remembered in hers. Whereas spectators brought in varied historical narratives about sugar, feelings can precede or subvert narrative; they are not assimilated by it. "Feelings can obviate the need for cognition, because feelings carry information. The discrete motions of our bodies convey how we are faring in the world," according to Jesse Prinz (Prinz 78). The feelings that found expression, from the ubiquitous "wow" to the panoply of responses that followed, carried a wealth of information about the status of cultural memory as it played out in the affectively anarchic space of Walker's installation.

Another reason that viewers had to absorb one another's reactions was the highly social nature of the visit for most. The vast majority of visitors arrived in groups or couples with the result that they articulated their feelings to one another within earshot of others. One walked out of the factory with the memory of far more than one's own response to the art since each viewer was subjected to the behaviors and observations of oth-ers. In a symbolic reflection of the molasses and sugar itself, then, view-ers registered sticky hands, sticky feet, and "sticky feelings" of the sphinx and molasses boys. "Sticky feelings" is a term that Sara Ahmed coined in order to explain that the "agency of emotions is not to be found in one place, within the self, or within the social" (Ahmed 89). Ahmed explains how certain signs—and she takes racial epithets as her example—accrue an "accumulation of affective value as a form of stickiness, or as sticky signs" (Ahmed 92). Sticky signs cannot be debunked through dualistic thinking, through a classic surface vs. depth analysis, to touch back on

Sedgwick.[18] "Rather than using stickiness to describe an object's surface, we can think of stickiness as an effect of surfacing, as an effect of the histories of contact between bodies, objects, and signs... stickiness depends on histories of contact that have already impressed upon the surface of the object" (Ahmed 90), and yet stickiness is not the property of an object. Rather, "it involves a transference of affect—a relation of 'doing' in which there is not a distinction between passive or active" (Ahmed 91). The divergent critical interpretations of the sphinx as an *objet d'art* demonstrate the indeterminacy of an object so firmly wedged into audience members' feelings about racial topoi and knowledge (or ignorance) of history. These feelings emerged from audience members into a shared affective space in which one viewer's grins and poses and another viewer's anger stuck to each other's psyches. Only the most glib of viewers could have passed through the space of the Domino factory without picking up a coating of some of this affective tension, for anyone who attributed any gravity to the sphinx, whether negative or positive, carried away the sticky feelings that clung to one's own sense of Walker's monument. In short, everyone exited the building with at least some attendant sense of others' responses to the art.

This transmission of affect, this "drama of contingency" (Ahmed 22), which occurs in work written about the installation as well as within its temporary space, is what underscores the work's function as a countermonument and its creation as such of affective archives. Whereas individual memories can be drawn on as archival materials, as we saw in earlier chapters, public art pushes individuals' feelings into the sphere of public record. Reactions can be literally recorded by those who witnessed them, and they continue to build and shift in subsequent memories and in photographs. While artist intentionality plays almost no role in the creation of this archive, Walker's contention that the history of sugar is inextricable from the history of slavery forms an underlying fact, in light of which the affective archive hinges on responses to bodies that represent slavery, in the labors of the molasses boys or in the sphinx's vulnerable sexual features and her "mammy" headdress, and in the sticky sweet medium in which they were formed. As Ahmed puts it, "to be affected by something is to evaluate that thing. Evaluations are expressed in how bodies turn toward things" (Ahmed 23). Glib responses were glib about slavery and racism; angry responses were angry about the racism that attended slavery and that gave rise to the racist stereotype of the hypersexual black woman; respectful responses remembered the pain and violence that fed the slave-dependent sugar industry from its inception. Again, Ahmed: "to experience an object as being affective or sensational is to be directed not only toward an object but to what is around that object, which includes what is behind the object, the conditions of its arrival" (Ahmed 25).

The myriad feelings about the sugar sculptures and their appearance in a sugar factory operational since the end of the Civil War in the biggest city in the United States provide a record of cultural memory about slavery in a way that no existing monument or memorial on US soil does. In fact, that is what the feelings laid bare: viewers had no shared understanding of the history of the sexualized black woman's body, lodged as that history is in centuries of exploitation and abuse by slave owners in the Americas and of a form of European exoticism born of colonial projections that culminated in a figure to which Walker alludes, that of Sara Baartman, colloquially known in the nineteenth century as the Hottentot Venus. Writing about Walker's use of stereotype alongside that of playwright Suzan-Lori Parks, Julie Burrell argues that the artists force confrontation with negative imagery because "instead of rehashing a formulation in which negative images are merely transformed into positive ones—a binary that could just as easily be reversed—their art forces audiences to dwell in the negative... [to] emerge not newly empowered but scathed" (Burrell 135). Burrell's emphasis on "scathing" is consistent with the point that several have made about such work in that it "position[s] affective response as the site of critique" (Burrell 135).

The problem as I've laid it out is that affective responses hinged at least in part on memory, and the amnesiac cultural memory that surfaced in the Domino plant clashed with the postmemories that it contained as well. They hinged as well on spectators' personal experiences of race in the U.S. or in other countries, experiences that diverge along lines that arguably do not meet in our current moment. As Morrison said, the entire point of a monumental site is to bring together personal memories with history in a form of felt knowledge. The countermonument, on the other hand, exposed felt knowledge along with felt ignorance and felt stuplimity. It also exposed the absence of recognition, the absence of a national site of remembrance and grieving for those who were conscribed to slavery—an absence born of an amnesia from which violence against black citizens continues to erupt in this country.

During the time that I was writing this chapter, The Museum of African American History and Culture opened on the National Mall in Washington, D.C. in the fall of 2016. Reviews indicate that this long-awaited museum forms an important site of remembrance and mourning, as well as recognition and celebration. In a preview, *The New York Times* identified the central question the curators and planners face thus: "How viscerally should the museum present the violence of slavery? So while shackles and a whip are shown, the exhibit on slave ships does not try to recreate the wretched conditions. Instead, visitors will see a few remnants—a pulley block used to hoist a sail or cargo and a piece of a hull from a Portuguese slave ship that sank off the coast of South Africa in 1794, taking 212 of the 500 slaves shackled on board to their deaths" (Bowley np). The museum includes as well the coffin of Emmett Till, an airplane flown by the Tuskeegee airmen, exhibits about the accomplishments of African Americans in music, politics, sports, and entertainment, a small display about the Obama presidency—and there was a last-minute rush to include an exhibit about the Black Lives Matter movement in response to the deaths of Eric Garner, Tamir Rice, Freddie Gray, Philando Castile, and the ever-growing number of African Americans who have died at the hands of the police in recent cultural memory. There is a chapel in the museum that is meant to be its memorial space, in that visitors are invited to use the room for quiet reflection and remembering. The question of whether the museum will do the same work as a memorial sculpture that could serve as a bench by the road in the nation's monument-strewn capital persists. The museum may be a much-needed *lieu de mémoire*, but while tickets for the museum are free, they are limited in number and reservations have to be made long in advance. The symbolic and affective power of a monument set in accessible, public space would enter into the narrative web created by the many memorials and monuments in the country that testify to different and sometimes clashing versions of history.

In the meantime, we have an instructive history of monuments, the affective responses they have elicited, and the *need* for sites of remembrance in the wake of Walker's sculpture. Although the sphinx has now given up the ghost, as it were, the feelings that she brought to the surface still simmer in the countless recordings and photographs of the installation and in what has been written about it. The sphinx now forms a *lieu de mémoire manqué*. Whether you were there to feel the overwhelming smell, tacky grit, and palpable clash of reactions that filled the Domino factory or not, the sphinx is, in true countermonumental fashion, an absent and haunting presence for all of us now. She leaves in her place an archive of sticky feelings (Fig. 4.1).

Fig. 4.1   Photo by Author

NOTES

1. As I write this, Hurricanes Irma and Maria have just destroyed much of St. Martin/ St. Maarten and I do not know the status of the monuments.
2. Also in New York, the United Nations erected a memorial in commemoration of the slave trade in 2015, a work that cannot be credited to the United States in spite of its location since it was supported by multiple nations and is not, technically, on U.S. soil.
3. And while the African Burial Ground monument is for the most part praised by critics, it was not without controversies surrounding the process, choice of artist and design, and sponsoring entities behind its production.
4. Pleasant's gravestone in Napa, California reads simply: "M.E.P. She was a friend of John Brown." The *Zong* was notorious because its crew threw 133 Africans overboard in order to claim insurance money upon their arrival in the Americas. Much has been written about the *Zong* by Caribbean writers like Cliff, Elizabeth Alexander, M. NourbeSe Philip, Fred d'Aguiar and others.
5. In another example of monumental erasure, Alan Rice offers a revealing statistic about the way in which plantation tours are conducted on those historically preserved in the United States: "there are thirty-one times as many mentions of furniture at these sites than of slavery or the enslaved" (Rice 10). He calls U.S. plantations "lieux d'oublier," or "sites of forgetting" in a play on Pierre Nora's "lieux de mémoire," or sites of memory.
6. At this moment it is almost impossible to keep up with the deluge of such cases in the news. Yale and Princeton have in the last year renamed houses and schools within the university, and Georgetown has been grappling with the revelation that it owes its survival to the sale of 272 slaves in 1838 to the harsh sugar plantations of Louisiana. Harvard convened a forum for scores of universities in the fall of 2016 to explore how to address their shared historical participation in slavery. Stories of the complicity of founders and universities in slavery are coming out of the woodwork this twenty-first century precisely because they have been successfully repressed for 150 years.
7. In the week that I am completing this book, plans for a memorial to the Charleston Emanuel A.M.E. Church victims and survivors have been unveiled. The figure of two soaring church pews in white, reminiscent of wings or of a ship's hull, may yet stand as a site of remembrance.
8. Symes was commenting on John Ahearn's "Bronx bronzes," three statues representing African Americans that were protested and taken down shortly after they went up. Ahearn's figures, of a young man in a hoodie crouched by a spike-collared pit bull, a pudgy middle-aged man leaning

on a boom box and holding a basketball, and a teenaged girl on roller skates, were deemed hurtful stereotypes.

9. A Philadelphia Soldiers and Sailors Monument that includes African Americans in both of those roles inspired debate as well, although the point of contention was not about the representational schema of the monument but rather about its location in the city. The monument was placed in a marginalized and run-down park, whereas as its proponents argued that it deserved a much more central and visible place in the city.

10. In her close reading of the memorial, Nora Faires points out some of the problems and paradoxes of the monument but she does not take issue with the figures themselves. See Nora Faires, "Across the Border to Freedom: The Underground Railroad Memorial and the Meanings of Migration." *Journal of American Ethnic History* 32.2 (2013): 38–67.

11. This pattern, of looking at how Holocaust remembrance informs cultural memory surrounding other historical traumas, is characteristic of literary as well as art historical analyses. Scholars argue for the application of that which they have learned through Holocaust studies to other events in several works, including Michael Rothberg's *Multidirectional Memory: Remembering the Holocaust in the Age of Decolonization* (Palo Alto: Stanford University Press, 2009), Debarati Sanayal's *Memory and Complicity: Migrations of Holocaust Remembrance* (New York: Fordham University Press, 2015) and Max Silverman's *Palimpsestic Memory: The Holocaust and Colonialism in French and Francophone Fiction and Film* (Brooklyn: Bergahn, 2013). Rothberg sets the stage for such studies by arguing that cultural memory had been organized in a "competitive" form whereby the remembrance of one group was paramount to forgetting others, and he shows how this form of memory is "exemplified in the presence of a Holocaust Museum and absence of a slavery museum in D.C.—and indeed these histories are often pitted against one another" (Rothberg 3). He theorizes a shift toward "non-competitive memory" through which remembrance of different histories coexists and complements one another. Silverman very much takes his cue from Rothberg in his argument that cultural memory is "palimpsestic," or that the focus on one event does not compete with but rather is layered with the multiple histories as they coexist in cultural memory, and Sanayal advances the value of "complicity," which she defines not as "a fixed stance but a structure of engagement that produces ethical and political reflection across proliferating frames of reference" (Sanayal 13). It is in the spirit of these studies that I draw on discussions of Holocaust memorialization from time to time.

12. Whereas I see a possible affective differential between monuments and memorials, in that monuments are potentially more celebratory and

memorials more somber in tone, I will reflect the critical terminology that uses both terms to discuss the larger exercise of commemoration in my discussion. I do find it interesting that Dr. Martin Luther King, Jr. was given a "monument" whereas Lincoln resides in a "memorial," and other such rhetorical distinctions in the genre, but that discussion is for another time.

13. Wilson goes on to note that Taylor's intent was not to represent the Middle Passage, but rather to speak to the changing ecosystem of the Caribbean. There are retractions of analyses of the sculpture as a Middle Passage memorial online, and most descriptions of the piece now make it clear that the piece is *not* about that historical event. It is interesting that critics and audiences are so eager to attribute truth to authorial intentions in this situation where the intentions serve to dismiss any allusion to slavery, whereas in other cases works are expected to speak for themselves. (The author has been "dead" since at least 1967.) Taylor's intentions relieve the viewer from the pain and anxiety that shackled figures on the floor of the sea might spark in those who contextualize his eco-art in the region's historical framework; moreover, he has said that he is open to interpretations of his work as a Middle Passage allusion even though that was not his own vision.

14. Walker has also commented that she owes her artistic career to having grown up in the shadow of the Stone Mountain Monument, a colossal Confederate monument carved into the side of a mountain in Georgia.

15. When I visited, I was stunned and horrified to see a group of European tourists posing in front of the breasts in a pose of nipple-tweaking—a pose that was performed repeatedly, as it turned out. Some of the sticky feelings that clung to me when I left were those of outrage at other viewers' ignorance and their inappropriate behavior. Like the notorious "Auschwitz selfie," a tweeted post of a teenager smiling in the midst of the camp at Auschwitz just weeks after Walker's installation closed, the photos that many took of the sphinx were deeply disrespectful at best and they lacked all historical context.

16. Katherine Brooks quotes Walker in her *Huffington Post* piece, "It Turns Out That Kara Walker and her Sugar Sphinx Were Watching Us the Whole Time."

17. Stephanye Watts, "The Audacity of No Chill: Kara Walker in the Instagram Capitol" (*Gawker*, June 6, 2014).

18. In this, Ahmed participates in Sedgwickian "reparative," as opposed to "paranoid" reading. Sedgwick takes critical inquiry to task for trying to "uncover violent or oppressive historical forces masquerading under liberal aesthetic guise" through critical practices aimed at "the topos of depth or hiddenness, typically followed by a drama of exposure" (Sedgwick 8). As a rejoinder to the failure of criticism that seeks out what

is "*beneath* or *behind*," Sedgwick proposes that affectively attuned critical strategies allow for the perception of meanings that lie *beside* one another. Besideness refuses dualistic thinking about surface and depth, subject and object, and so on, and "comprises a wide range of desiring, identifying, representing, repelling, paralleling, differentiating, reviling, leaning, twisting, mimicking, withdrawing, attracting, aggressing, warping, and other relations" (Sedgwick 8).

CHAPTER 5

Coda: On Memory and Memorial

Abstract In this brief coda, I bring the reader up to speed on the rapidly changing memorial landscape of 2018 as a follow-up to the previous chapter on countermonuments. In the years and even months preceding the completion of this book, significant memorial work has been done in the United States and abroad in the larger project of commemorating the lives of the enslaved. I use the timely and continuing conversation around memorialization to reconnect to the ways in which writers have theorized and practiced public feelings in various forms of memoir-work.

Keywords Monuments · Memorials · Cultural memory · Reparative reading

I started writing this book around the summer of 2015 and it has since taken on cultural resonances that I could never have foreseen but that I will try to address in this brief coda. What began as an academic inquiry into affect theory and the uses of memory became a book whose defining chapter is likely, in the current climate of 2018, to be the one that deals with monuments and memorials. This is the case because, as I note in Chapter 1, the United States is embroiled in a heated debate about the role of monuments in public space in the wake of the deadly violence that erupted last summer around hate groups rallying to defend a monument of Robert E. Lee that was slated for removal. Such removals are

© The Author(s) 2018
E. L. Johnson, *Cultural Memory, Memorials, and Reparative
Writing*, Palgrave Studies in Affect Theory and Literary Criticism,
https://doi.org/10.1007/978-3-030-02098-9_5

continuing, if at a much more sluggish pace than in 2017, so the conversation remains timely. For that reason, this coda will attend to the topic of memorialization in the process of drawing conclusions about how personal and cultural memory function as archival and affective forces in literature, theory, and culture.

In the months leading up to the writing of this conclusion, one of the most raw and powerful monuments to deal with racial violence in the United States opened: The Peace and Justice Memorial in Montgomery, Alabama. This sprawling, harrowing structure memorializes the 4,384 documented lynchings committed during the period following the Civil War. While lynchings are the central topic of the piece, the memorial places them in historical context in its scope "From Enslavement to Mass Incarceration." Financed and organized by the Alabama-based Equal Justice Initiative, the memorial's central structure is an immense, square roof-like plane from which hang 816 massive iron plinths inscribed with the names of victims by county. The site is so vast that it resists photography in an age of selfies and cellphone cameras. It demands to be visited, both by the nature of its immersive design and by the 816 duplicate planks that lie on the ground surrounding the monument, waiting to be claimed and placed as memorials within the counties where the commemorated atrocities against African American men and women took place. This aspect of the memorial—that it might proliferate 816 sister memorials around the country—is among its most transformative effects.[1] This single act of commemoration has the potential to significantly alter the landscape of cultural memory in the United States. I have not yet made the trip and will have to imagine the soul-searing pain the space stirs up and the weight and danger viewers must feel hanging over their heads as they pass beneath the suspended blocks that would crush them, were they to fall. The personal accounts of visits I have heard speak of intense experiences of sorrow and shame. One visitor notes Montgomery's history of non-violent protest and says that, "In this case the protest is not for rights but for memory" (Candler 22). Similarly, journalist Jamelle Bouie writes, "a memorial to racial terrorism—one which indicts perpetrators as much as it honors victims—is the kind of provocation that we need, a vital and powerful statement against our national tendency to willful amnesia" (Bouie np). In effect, the site is a colossal installation of memory.

It is also the most frank address in the country to its history of enslavement and racial violence. The Peace and Justice Memorial is an astonishing accomplishment in a national landscape that still bristles with monuments to the Confederacy and remains relatively empty of those to generations of its victims. As numerous commentators including the memorial's visionary, Bryan Stevenson, have pointed out, the United States is in need of a truth and reconciliation movement—one that cannot occur without first facing the truth of its history.

The swirl of powerful and often devastating feelings provoked by the memorial is inseparable from the cultural memory it instills in its viewers. In this, its effect is to illustrate the importance of affective knowledge as it is prompted by memorial art. However, beyond the Peace and Justice Memorial and a few of the monuments I detailed in the previous chapter, we have to look outside of the United States for additional examples of monuments and memorials that do this kind of work. As I note in the chapter on countermemorials, Caribbean countries have perhaps the strongest records on commemoration. In addition to the memorials, in St. Martin, Barbados, Martinique, Jamaica, St. Thomas, St. Croix, and Guyana to which I allude in that chapter, one of the most recent additions to this genre of remembrance was unveiled in Barbados in 2013. Entitled "Quaw's Quest," after Quaw Williams who was 37 at the time of emancipation and went on to achieve an advanced degree and leadership in his community, the memorial is a thorough engagement with the history of the enslaved as it overlapped with the Cave Hill campus of the University of the West Indies where it is located. The piece is an assemblage of a figural sculpture, tablets inscribed with Quaw's accomplishments and vision of justice, and enormous ledgers bearing the names of each of the 294 slaves who were living on what is now the campus grounds, at the time of emancipation. This combination of so many different elements in a singular effort of commemoration resonates with the Peace and Justice Memorial which also features figural art, text-based historical records, and symbolic forms. The three ledgers of "Quaw's Quest" face out to the sea in much the same way that the somber stone people of Martinique's *Cap 110* do. They list names, ages, race ("black" or "coloured"), and work assignments ("domestic" or "laborer"). As with the Peace and Justice Memorial, this restoration of names works as a crucial intervention in an archive replete with nameless people, in a history of stolen lives. Moreover, the ledger is a powerful symbol of the archive of slavery given the troves of ships' logs that recorded the existence of the enslaved while simultaneously discharging their humanity from such records.[2] Thus the textual elements of both pieces remediate the archive in a quite direct manner while the emotional impact that reflecting on individual lives has on viewers effects historical knowledge on a personal level.

Another monument that has just gone up in the months before this book goes to press is Denmark's "Queen Mary," located in Copenhagen. In April of 2018, Crucian artist La Vaughn Belle and Danish artist Jeanette Ehlers unveiled an extraordinary figure of strength, beauty, and nobility in the figure of Mary Thomas, one of several fabled black women who led a wide-reaching revolt, "Fireburn," in nineteenth-century Danish St. Croix. She sits atop a tall pillar in a wicker chair with a fan back that, along with her pose, alludes to the iconic 1967 photograph of Huey Newton. Like Newton, she holds two objects out in front of her—in her case, a torch and a sugar cane cutting tool. The memorial landscape is thus shifting around the Atlantic, as Françoise Vergès argues when she says, "en effet, peu de descendants de négriers ou d'esclavagistes ont réclamé un devoir de mémoire. Par contre, des *villes négriers*—Liverpool, Bristol, Nantes, ou Bordeaux—ont été amenées par des associations" (Vergès 156) [in effect, few descendants of the enslaved or of slave holders have laid claim to the burden of memory. In contrast, port cities of the slave trade—Liverpool, Bristol, Nantes, or Bordeaux—have led with various associations]. While Vergès does not take the Caribbean into consideration in this comment, which she makes in the context of a collection of essays about France's "memory wars," her point about the port cities is well taken. For example, Liverpool's International Slavery Museum opened its doors in 2007 and is organized around the three foci of life in pre-colonial West Africa, the Middle Passage, and the ongoing legacy of racial discrimination and of African Diasporic contributions to Western culture. The museum also features a "Freedom Sculpture" made by Haitian artists Mario Benjamin, Eugène, Céleur, and Guyodo out of recycled materials.

I am not artistic enough to suggest a counter/monument in form, and I appreciate skepticism around the phenomenon of national monuments as effective articulations of history, but whether it is a bench by the road, a composite of textual, figural, and symbolic forms, or a tribute to the constant resistance practiced by the enslaved, I still hope to see a nationally funded monument in Washington, D.C., recognizing the history of slavery and in memory of the enslaved. My hope is that detailing other successful examples can contribute in some way to a material marker there.

And to return to the question of why monuments matter we can travel back to the intertwining forces of affect and memory that they compel. Sedgwick herself reflects on sculpture in her book that guides much of this one, *Touching Feeling*. She looks at the complex, heterogeneous, body-sized bundles of sculptor Judith Scott, and sees the "besideness" of the artist and her art. That is, rather than seeing a subject–object relationship between the two, Sedgwick's view takes in the extent to which the artist's creation continues to affect her sensory subjectivity. Sculptures, whether made of textiles, stone, or sugar, are not just objective presences once the artist puts on her finishing touches; they are part of the weave of our landscapes, cityscapes, and culturescapes. Sedgwick links her concept of besideness to Deleuze and Guattari's "interest in planar relations," explaining that "the irreducibly spatial positionality of *beside* also seems to offer some useful resistance to the ease with which *beneath* and *beyond* turn from spatial descriptors into implicit narratives of, respectively, origin and telos" (Sedgwick 8). She invokes Deleuze and Guattari's concept of the rhizome here, and indeed when we consider our relationship to public art as one of "besideness" we assume a rhizomatic stance through which we are implicated not only in the art's meaning, but in its very presence in shared space. In the metaphor of the rhizome, a plant that grows often horizontally and sends out shoots at random nodes, collapsing any distinction between roots and branches, we exist in a field of interlocking meanings generated by multiple points of reference. Beyond her close reading of how Scott and her art form such an interlocking relationship, Sedgwick's inquiry concerns how we might live with everything from art objects to social phenomena in a reparative manner, in a way that is "additive and accretive" (Sedgwick 149). She prompts her readers to think about how we absorb historical and cultural meaning into ourselves, and how we hold it there.

The original and admittedly overly academic title for this book was "The Affective Archive." But the idea behind that term is that affective conditions of being in the world are sources of knowledge about it, and that memory work is a way of reaching into those reservoirs of information. The fact that affect studies has developed as a discrete methodology, and that so many writers in the field have been drawing on their own memories in the course of cultural and intellectual analysis echoes the strategies of memoirists who link their experiences to archival materials and cultural memory. Academic writing in the humanities and social sciences is trending toward this more personal voice across the board;

certainly literary and cultural critics have in recent years drawn on personal feelings and memories in a way that the pre-internet, print-based version of criticism did not. In light of this trend within and beyond academic writing, we should be ever attentive to the ways in which cultural memory can remediate incomplete histories and archives and become yet another archival source in the field of cultural understanding. This intellectual shift could also be framed as a response to Sedgwick's call in 2003 when she expressed concern about the "paranoid" nature of critical writing. She was troubled that the drive toward explicating and debunking, rather than living with and thinking though social problems, resulted from a self-fulfilling methodological prophecy. Her move toward reparative reading requires more capacious and experimental forms of writing, insofar as "the vocabulary for articulating any reader's reparative motive toward a text or a culture has long been so sappy, aestheticizing, defensive, anti-intellectual, or reactionary that it's no wonder few critics are willing to describe their acquaintance with such motives. The prohibitive problem, however, has been in the limitations of present theoretical vocabularies rather than in the reparative motive itself" (Sedgwick 150). This is why the reparative writing of the theorists and memoirists I have covered in this book is so important: they are finding new vocabularies for not just thinking through the history of racial injustice and myriad other social difficulties but for *being* in them, for living in them. As Claudia Rankine writes in *Citizen: An American Lyric*, we are "still in the difficulty."[3]

NOTES

1. One of the first communities to claim their plinth was Duluth, Minnesota, a town that already houses a major monument to three men who were lynched there in the early twentieth century and that has therefore not shied away from their history of violence.
2. In his novel *The Feeding of Ghosts*, Fred d'Aguiar also makes the ledger a central symbol in his telling of the notorious story of the *Zong* tragedy.
3. I am indebted to Wendy Walters for highlighting the power of Rankine's line in her essay, "'Still in the Difficulty': The Afterlives of Archives." *Memory as Colonial Capital: Cross-Cultural Conversations in French and English*, eds. Erica L. Johnson and Éloïse Brezault (New York and London: Palgrave Macmillan, 2017).

WORKS CITED

Abraham, Nicolas and Maria Torok. *The Shell and the Kernel: Renewals in Psychoanalysis*. Chicago: University of Chicago Press, 1994.

Ahmed, Sara. *The Cultural Politics of Emotion*. Edinburgh: Edinburgh University Press, 2004.

Als, Hilton. "The Sugar Sphinx." *The New Yorker* (May 8, 2014).

Anzaldùa, Gloria. *Borderlands/La Frontera: The New Mestiza*. San Francisco: Aunt Lute Books, 2012.

Ater, Renée. "Slavery and Its Memory in Public Monuments." *American Art* 24.1 (2010): 20–23.

———. *Remaking Race and History: The Sculpture of Meta Warrick Fuller*. Berkeley: University of California Press, 2011.

Becze, Ayn. "Review of *A Map to the Door of No Return: Notes to Belonging*." *Canadian Ethnic Studies* 35.1 (2003).

Berlant, Lauren. *Cruel Optimism*. Durham and London: Duke University Press, 2011.

———. "Claudia Rankine." *BOMB* 129 (Fall 2014).

Bernier, Celeste-Marie and Hannah Durkin, eds. *Visualizing Slavery: Art Across the African Diaspora*. Liverpool: Liverpool University Press, 2016.

Bernier, Celeste-Marie and Judie Newman. *Public Art, Memorials and Atlantic Slavery*. New York and London: Routledge, 2009.

Bold, Christine, Ric Knowles, and Belinda Leach. "How Might a Women's Monument Be Different?" *Essays on Canadian Writing* 80 (2003): 17–35.

© The Editor(s) (if applicable) and The Author(s) 2018
E. L. Johnson, *Cultural Memory, Memorials, and Reparative Writing*,
Palgrave Studies in Affect Theory and Literary Criticism,
https://doi.org/10.1007/978-3-030-02098-9

Booth, Marilyn. "Fiction's Imaginative Archive and the Newpaper's Local Scandals." *Archive Stories: Facts, Fictions, and the Writing of History*. Ed. Antoinette Burton. Durham and London: Duke University Press, 2005.

Bouie, Jamelle. "The Pain We Still Need to Feel." *Slate* (May 1, 2018).

Bowley, Graham. "How Do You Tell the Story of Black America in One Museum?" *The New York Times* (March 26, 2016).

Brand, Dionne. *A Map to the Door of No Return: Notes on Belonging*. Toronto: Doubleday Canada, 2001.

Brennan, Teresa. *The Transmission of Affect*. Ithaca: Cornell University Press, 2004.

Brooks, Katherine. "It Turns Out That Kara Walker and Her Sugar Sphinx Were Watching Us the Whole Time." *Huffington Post* (November 14, 2014).

Bruyneel, Kevin. "The King's Body: The Martin Luther King, Jr. Memorial and the Politics of Collective Memory." *History and Memory* 26.1 (2014): 75–108.

Burrell, Julie. "The Lower Stratus of History: The Grotesque Comic Stereotypes of Suzan-Lori Parks and Kara Walker." *Imagining the Black Female Body*. Ed. Carol Henderson. New York: Palgrave Macmillan, 2010.

Candler, Pete. "Names of the Lynched: A Visit to the National Memorial for Peace and Justice." *Christian Century* (June 20, 2018).

Caruth, Cathy. *Unclaimed Experience: Trauma, Narrative, and Experience*. Baltimore: Johns Hopkins University Press, 1994.

Chamoiseau, Patrick and Rodolphe Hammadi. *Guyane: Traces-mémoires du bagne*. Paris: Caisse nationale des monuments et sites historiques, 1994.

Cho, Grace. *Haunting the Korean Diaspora: Shame, Secrecy, and the Forgotten War*. Minneapolis: University of Minnesota Press, 2008.

Cliff, Michelle. *Free Enterprise*. San Francisco: City Lights Books, 2004.

Clough, Patricia Ticinto. *Autoaffection: Unconscious Thought in the Age of Technology*. Minneapolis: University of Minnesota Press, 2000.

Clough, Patricia Ticinto and Jean Halley, eds. *The Affective Turn: Theorizing the Social*. Durham and London: Duke University Press, 2007.

Cooks, Bridget R. "Activism and Preservation: Fred Wilson's *E Pluribus Unum*." *Indiana Magazine of History* 110 (2014): 25–31.

Crownshaw, Richard. *The Afterlife of Holocaust Memory in Contemporary Literature and Culture*. New York: Palgrave Macmillan, 2010.

Cvetkovich, Ann. *An Archive of Feelings: Trauma, Sexuality, and Lesbian Public Cultures*. Durham and London: Duke University Press, 2003.

———. *Depression: A Public Feeling*. Durham and London: Duke University Press, 2012.

Deleuze, Gilles and Félix Guattari. *One Thousand Plateaus: Capitalism and Schizophrenia*. Minneapolis: University of Minnesota Press, 1987.

Denzin, Norman K. *Interpretive Autoethnography.* Thousand Oaks, CA: Sage, 2013.

Derrida, Jacques. *Archive Fever: A Freudian Impression.* Trans. Eric Prenowitz. Chicago: University of Chicago Press, 1996.

Diehl, Carol. "Dirty Sugar: Kara Walker's Dubious Alliance with Domino." *Black Renaissance Noire* (2014): 94–95.

Doss, Erika. *Memorial Mania: Public Feeling in America.* Chicago: University of Chicago Press, 2012.

———. "Public Art, Public Response: Negotiating Civic Shame in Duluth, Minnesota." *Indiana Magazine of History* 110 (2014): 40–46.

DuBois Shaw, Gwendolyn. *Seeing the Unspeakable: The Art of Kara Walker.* Durham: Duke University Press, 2004.

Edenheim, Sara. "Lost and Never Found: The Queer Archive of Feelings and Its Historical Propriety." *Differences* 24.3 (2013): 36–62.

Eichhorn, Kate. *The Archival Turn in Feminism: Outrage in Order.* Philadelphia: Temple University Press, 2014.

Erll, Astrid and Ann Regney. *Mediation, Remediation, and the Dynamics of Cultural Memory.* Berlin: DeGruyter, 2009.

Fabre, Geneviève and Robert O'Meally. *History and Memory in African-American Culture.* New York and Oxford: Oxford University Press, 1994.

Finkelpearl, Tom. *Dialogues in Public Art: Interviews with Vito Acconci, John Ahearn.* Cambridge: MIT Press, 2000.

Forsdick, Charles. 2015. "Travel, Slavery, Memory: Thanatourism in the French Atlantic." *Postcolonial Studies* 17 (3): 251–265.

Fournier, Jean-Pierre. *La Guyane ou les réalités du bagne.* Paris: Beau Livre, 2007.

Gordon, Avery. *Ghostly Matters: Haunting and the Sociological Imagination.* Minneapolis: University of Minnesota Press, 1997.

Graves, James Blau. *Cultural Democracy: The Arts, Community, and the Public Purpose.* Urbana: University of Illinois Press, 2004.

Gregg, Melissa. *Cultural Studies' Affective Voices.* New York and London: Palgrave Macmillan, 2006.

Halley, Jean O'Malley. *The Parallel Lives of Women and Cows: Meat Markets.* New York: Palgrave Macmillan, 2012.

Harrison, Paul Carter. "Preamble to Kara Walker's Tragi-comedy." *Black Renaissance Noire* (2014).

Henke, Suzette. *Shattered Subjects: Trauma and Testimony in Women's Life-Writing.* New York: Palgrave Macmillan, 2000.

Hirsch, Marianne. *Family Frames: Photography, Narrative, and Postmemory.* New York: CreateSpace Independent Publishing, 2012.

James, Owain and Joanne Garde-Hansen. *Geography and Memory.* New York and London: Palgrave Macmillan, 2012.

Johnson, Erica L. "Review of *The Parallel Lives of Women and Cows: Meat Markets*, Jean O'Malley Halley." *Qualitative Inquiry* (July 4, 2016). https://doi.org/10.1177/1077800416657100.

Knepper, Wendy. *Patrick Chamoiseau: A Critial Introduction*. Jacksonville: University of Mississippi Press, 2012.

Labode, Modupe. "Guest Editor's Introduction." *Indiana Magazine of History* 110 (2014): 1–8.

Landrieu, Mitch. "Mitch Landrieu's Speech on the Removal of Confederate Monuments in New Orleans." *The New York Times* (May 23, 2017).

Loichot, Valérie. "Kara Walker's Blood Sugar: *A Subtlety or the Marvelous Sugar Baby*." *Southern Spaces* (July 8, 2014).

Lorde, Audre. *Sister Outsider*. New York: Crossing Press Feminist Series, 2007.

Love, Heather. *Feeling Backward: Loss and the Politics of Queer History*. Cambridge: Harvard University Press, 2009.

———. "Truth and Consequences: On Paranoid Reading and Reparative Reading." *Criticism* 52.2 (2010): 235–241.

Mason, Jody. "Searching for the 'Doorway': Dionne Brand's *Thirsty*." *University of Toronto Quarterly* 75.2 (2006).

Massumi, Brian. "The Autonomy of Affect." *Cultural Critique* 31 (1995): 83–109.

McCalebb, Howard. "Apoplexy: The Furor Over Kara Walker." *Kara Walker-No/Kara Walker-Yes/Kara Walker-?* Ed. Pindell Howardena. New York: Midmarch Arts Press, 2009.

McCusker, Maeve. *Patrick Chamoiseau: Recovering Memory*. Liverpool: Liverpool University Press, 2007.

McKay, Nellie Y. "Washington Park." *History and Memory in African-American Culture*. Ed. Geneviève Fabre and Robert O'Meally. New York and Oxford: Oxford University Press, 1994.

Mintz, Stanley. *Sweetness and Power: The Place of Sugar in Modern History*. New York: Penguin, 1986.

Mitter, Siddharta. "The Artist and the Revolutionary." *The Village Voice* (September 5, 2017).

Morrison, Toni. "Unspeakable Things Unspoken." *The Tanner Lectures on Human Values*. University of Michigan, 1988.

Moynagh, Maureen. "The Melancholic Structure of Memory in Dionne Brand's *The Full and Change of the Moon*." *Journal of Commonwealth Literature* 43.1 (2008): 57–75.

Ngai, Sianne. *Ugly Feelings*. Cambridge and London: Harvard University Press, 2005.

Nora, Pierre. *Les Lieux de mémoire*. Paris: Gallimard, 1993.

Nyong'o, Tavia. *The Amalgamation Waltz: Race, Performance, and the Ruses of Memory*. Minneapolis: University of Minnesota Press, 2009.

Orr, Jackie. *Panic Diaries: A Genealogy of Panic Disorder.* Durham and London. Duke University Press, 2006.

Osbey, Brenda Marie. "Note to Clyde Taylor." *Black Renaissance Noire* (2014): 96.

Parham, Marisa. "Hughes, Cullen, and the In-sites of Loss." *ELH* 74.2 (2007): 429–447.

Pindell, Howardena, ed. *Kara Walker-No/Kara Walker-Yes/Kara Walker-?* New York: Midmarch Arts Press, 2009.

Prinz, Jesse. *Gut Reactions.* Oxford: Oxford University Press, 2006.

Probyn, Elspeth. *Blush: Faces of Shame.* Minneapolis: University of Minnesota Press, 2005.

Rice, Alan. *Creating Memorials, Building Identities: The Politics of Memory in the Black Atlantic.* Liverpool: Liverpool University Press, 2010.

———. "A Home for Ourselves in the World: Caryl Philips on Slave Forts and Manillas as African Atlantic Sites of Memory." *Atlantic Studies* 9.3 (2012): 363–372.

Rothberg, Michael. *Multidirectional Memory: Remembering the Holocaust in the Age of Decolonization.* Palo Alto: Stanford University Press, 2009.

———. "Introduction: Between Memory and Memory: From *Lieux de mémoire* to *Noeuds de mémoire.*" *Yale French Studies* 118/119 (2010): 3–12.

Russell, Francey. "A Subtlety at the Domino Factory: Kara Walker." *LA Review of Books* (June 20, 2014).

Sanyal, Debarati. *Memory and Complicity: Migrations of Holocaust Remembrance.* New York: Fordham, 2015.

Savage, Kirk. *Standing Soldiers, Kneeling Slaves: Race, War, and Monument in 19th-Century America.* Princeton: Princeton University Press, 1999.

———. *Monument Wars: Washington D.C., The National Mall, and the Transformation of the Memorial Landscape.* Berkeley: University of California Press, 2011.

Savali, Kristen West. "From Mammy to the Marvelous Sugar Baby: The Art of Black Womanhood." *The Huffington Post* (June 10, 2014).

Scott, Joan. "The Evidence of Experience." *Feminist Approaches to Theory and Methodology: An Interdisciplinary Reader.* Eds. Sharlene Hesse-Biber, Christina GIlmartin, and Robin Lydenberg. New York and Oxford: Oxford University Press, 1999.

Sedgwick, Eve Kosofsky. *Touching Feeling: Affect, Pedagogy, Performativity.* London and Durham: Duke University Press, 2003.

Silverman, Max. "Trips, Tropes and Traces: Reflections on Memory in French and Francophone Culture." *Anamnesia: Private and Public Memory in Modern French Culture.* Eds. Peter Collier, Anna Magdalena Elsner, and Olga Smith. New York: Peter Lang, 2009.

———. "Memory Traces: Patrick Chamoiseau and Rodolphe Hammadi's *Guyane: Traces-mémoires du bagne.*" *Yale French Studies* 118/119 (2010): 225–238.

————. *Palimpsestic Memory: The Holocaust and Colonialism in French and Francophone Fiction and Film.* Oxford and New York: Berghahn, 2013.

Smith, Roberta. "Sugar? Sure, but Salted with Meaning." *The New York Times* (May 11, 2014).

Stewart, Kathleen. *Ordinary Affects.* Durham and London: Duke University Press, 2007.

Stoler, Laura Ann. *Carnal Knowledge and Imperial Power: Race and the Intimate in Colonial Rule.* Berkeley, Los Angeles and London: University of California Press, 2002.

Taylor, Clyde. "Preamble to Kara Walker Tragicomedy." *Black Renaissance Noire* (2014): 93.

Thomas, Hank Willis. "The Overwhelming Whiteness of Black Art." Jamilah King. *ColorLines* (May 21, 2014).

Thrift, Nigel. *Non-Representational Theory: Space, Politics, Affect.* Hoboken: Taylor and Francis, 2007.

Tinsley, Omise'eke Natasha. "Black Atlantic, Queer Atlantic: Queer Imaginings of the Middle Passage." *GLQ* 14.2–3 (2008): 191–212.

Toth, Stephen A. *Beyond Papillon: The French Overseas Penal Colonies 1854–1952.* Lincoln: University of Nebraska Press, 2006.

Vergès, Françoise. "Esclavage colonial: quelles mémoires? Quels héritages?" *Les Guerres de mémoires.* Eds. Pascale Blanchard and Isabelle Veyrat-Masson. Paris: La Découverte, 2008.

Wainwright, Leon. "Art and Caribbean Slavery: Modern Visions of the 1763 Guyana Rebellion." *Visualizing Slavery: Art Across the African Diaspora.* Eds. Bernier, Celeste-Marie and Hannah Durkin. Liverpool: Liverpool University Press, 2016.

Walker, Kara. "Kara Walker Secretly Filmed You Taking Selfies in Front of Her Sphinx." *Vulture* (November 19, 2014).

————. "Sweet Talk." Radcliffe Institute for Advanced Study, Harvard University, Cambridge, MA (December 14, 2014).

Walker, Kara and Jad Abumrad. "New York Public Library Interview." (May 20, 2014).

Whitney, Shiloh. "Affective Indigestion: Lorde, Fanon, and Gutierrez-Rodriguez on Race and Affective Labor." *Journal of Speculative Philosophy* 30.3 (2016): 278–291.

Wickham, Kim. "'I Undo You, Master': Uncomfortable Encounters in the Work of Kara Walker." *The Comparatist* 39 (2015): 335–354.

Wilson, Fred. "Inspirations." *Indiana Magazine of History* 110 (2014): 10–24.

Wood, Marcus. *Blind Memory: Visual Representations of Slavery in England and America, 1780–1865.* New York and London: Routledge, 2000.

Young, James E. *The Texture of Memory: Holocaust Memorials and Meaning.* New Haven: Yale University Press, 1994.

INDEX

© The Editor(s) (if applicable) and The Author(s) 2018   107
E. L. Johnson, *Cultural Memory, Memorials, and Reparative Writing*,
Palgrave Studies in Affect Theory and Literary Criticism,
https://doi.org/10.1007/978-3-030-02098-9

Printed by Printforce, the Netherlands